A BIRD'S EYE VIEW

Insights and experiences from
professional women

Sarah Snell

2000

First published in 2002 by Management Books 2000 Ltd
Forge House, Limes Road
Kemble, Cirencester
Gloucestershire, GL7 6AD, UK
Tel: 0044 (0) 1285 771441/2
Fax: 0044 (0) 1285 771055
E-mail: m.b.2000@virgin.net
Web: mb2000.com

Printed and bound in Great Britain by Biddles, Guildford

British Library Cataloguing in Publication Data is available

ISBN 1-85252-406-5

Contents

Acknowledgements

This book owes its origins to Kim Wain who I must thank for planting the idea of talking to senior women in business as part of a plan to establish what I wanted to do next. Having talked it through with a number of people, it became clear to me that there were many more women who needed similar sources of advice and insight, and so the project took off.

Unreserved thanks go to all the business women and undergraduates who agreed to be interviewed and whose insights form the body of this book. Their honesty and desire to help others, together with the time taken out of busy schedules, sets them apart as role models for many others.

The initial outline of the project, together with some of the early interviews, was done in collaboration with Louise Makin. Without her regular phone calls to see how I was getting on and to reaffirm the need for the book, I would never have got this far. Thanks also go to Louise and to friends and family for their feedback on the final draft - their enthusiastic interest, feedback and constructive criticism at various stages have been an important motivator in completing the project.

Chapter One

Making It Happen

This book sets out to provide a practical guide for professional women based on the learning and experiences of some of the most successful women leaders in British business. It does not present theories or statistical evidence to prove or disprove how some women become top performers – rather it offers the opinions, thoughts and experiences of those women themselves.

For many of us, there are very few role models in our world of work who we can look to for advice. 'A Bird's Eye View' draws on detailed face-to-face interviews, providing a privileged insight. In contrast to much of the literature which urges industry leaders and organisations to remove the 'glass ceiling' and become a female-friendly environment, this guide focuses on the individual who wants to manage the reality of the present and offers advice to those impatient for the business and social changes to occur around them. Interestingly, none of the women interviewed recognised the glass ceiling as an issue for themselves as they felt acknowledging such a concept created an artificial barrier. Whilst unquestionably many had encountered subtle and overt discriminating behaviour along the way, they had not allowed it to impede their progress and had adopted the simple tactic of ignoring it to focus on the bigger issues or by changing organisation.

Context

In my experience, there is a shortage of practical advice and guidance for women during their careers to balance the off-putting sensationalist stereotyping that ascribes superwoman or she-devil status to those who succeed. The businesswomen who receive media coverage are often represented as extremes and obscure a multitude of options for professional women.

Previous generations of women were educated to achieve in the business world yet socially conditioned to understand that this would probably require a willingness to adapt to other peoples' terms and values. Often these were represented by the informal, unspoken rules of an organisation.

Women today are educated to believe they can achieve anything they want and that they operate on a level playing field. They are conditioned to be independent and demanding and are not prepared to compromise if it means a shift away from their personal values.

However, for professional women progressing in a business career, there is an acute awareness that the reality is not so straightforward and often this leads to conflict. In many cases, this realisation comes when they start a family, in others it arises from a difference in values with the organisation or an unwillingness to continue to be 'one of the boys'.

Undoubtedly, there are now more women in business and at senior levels than twenty years ago. However, women are still woefully under-represented in many industries and organisations. An Institute of Management survey reported that only 24% of British managers are women with the number dwindling to less than 10% in Engineering and in terms of equal pay, female directors still only receive around 85% of the equivalent male salary[1]. The reality is that this will take time to change as younger generations of women make their way through their career paths and the social climate changes to make it easier for men to stay at home and play a larger role in childcare and domestic responsibilities. The issue is not so much about making things better for women as about enabling modern men and women to make the decisions that are right for them.

Individuals are also starting to question whether the traditional model of being successful in business is really what they want in the light of the lifestyle sacrifices that are required. KPMG[2] found that the business leaders of today are unhappy about the amount of time they spend away from home whilst female undergraduates interviewed for this book were already considering whether their career choices would enable them to have flexible working patterns at various stages of their working lives.

Whilst organisations and industry may aspire to be different – and many have recognised the need for change – a shift in attitudes and behaviours does not occur overnight. Many companies have introduced policies to address the issue.

---

1. **Institute of Management survey as reported in "The Management Today Global Salary Survey", August 2001**
2. **KPMG Business Leadership Survey 1999**

However, few are consistently put into practice. This results in a disconnect between the intentions of a business and the actual experiences of the women who work. A report by Saxton and Bamfylde[3] introduces the concept of 'gender blindness' to indicate sectors where gender is less of an issue.

'Some sectors are more gender blind than others. Among the favourites are media organisations and the civil service. Sectors with strong software and intellectual property components tend to be more used to women and more able to value women's traditional strengths such as the 'soft skills' of interpretation and intuitive insight.'

This is reflected in how some younger women are making their choices. In addition to interviews with successful businesswomen, interviews were also conducted with female final-year undergraduates about to embark on their careers. One opted for the research side of corporate banking – still a demanding role but perceived as much less aggressive and more collaborative than the trading side of the business. The environment was more appealing to her than one of continual and intensive one-upmanship and competition. Another opted for the Bar rather than a career as a solicitor because she felt the self-employment option would allow her more control and flexibility in the long term to take time out to accomplish her ambition of writing a book.

In more traditional environments, the issue of senior women in an organisation can present a fundamental challenge. There are often very strongly held personal prejudices that take significant time and work to change. High achieving women in

3. **"Glass Ceilings or Mirrors", Saxton Bamfylde Hever plc, October 1999**

those environments cannot afford to wait for that change to happen and can benefit from the guidance of the select group who went before them.

Trends in the workplace

Whilst there has been a significant increase in the number of professional women, it is still only a small number who reach the top of their chosen professions. Today, the changing nature of the working environment provides an extra stimulus for understanding why this may be.

A number of trends are currently being hotly debated including the increasing impact of technology, the long-hours culture, the dissatisfaction with work/life balance, the change in the traditional family unit, the disappearance of job security, and the leadership challenges in highly dynamic and ever changing markets. Clearly, these are issues for all employees whatever their gender but raise particular questions and opportunities for professional women.

There are many women who have left traditional organisations to become entrepreneurs, allowing themselves to establish a business that has values and unspoken rules with which they feel more comfortable and which allow a more flexible approach. They work as hard as they did before but in a way that enables them to manage their professional aspirations and other aspects of their life more effectively. It is also interesting to note that women run a quarter of SMEs in this country. Why are they so much more successful and visible here than in large corporates?

Another factor to consider is the well-documented trend for women to become more independent professionally, financially and socially and the ESRC's report, '*Britain towards 2010: the changing business environment'*[4] forecasts this trend to continue. Increasingly, the media are profiling women who combine study with maternity leave, women who are the main income earners or the rise in numbers of single professional women.

The report also predicts a need for organisations to change their structures, encourage more innovation, recognise higher job fluidity and promote less management control, to be competitive in the business environment of the 21st century. As a result, individuals, both male and female, will have to negotiate hard, learn to self-promote and focus on self-development. The net outcome is that the environment we operate in will become less secure and less constant, requiring individuals to take more control. It will be less and less common for individuals to have followed a traditional career path with no breaks in their working life. These changes should prove advantageous for women in allowing them to have greater flexibility in how they manage careers and motherhood. However, other, more fundamental, shifts will need to take place to facilitate this. Despite recent social changes incorporating parental leave and in some instances paternity pay, it is still women in the majority of cases who take the career break and stay at home. More and more men would like to consider this option but the social climate still makes it difficult for them to do so.

'Although they are taking more responsibility for bringing up their children because of the steady increase in working mothers, they are afraid that raising the issue of childcare at work will penalise their careers.' [5]

---

4. **"Britain towards 2010: the changing business environment", Richard Scase, Economic and Social Research Council, August 1999.**
5. **The Times, 9th May 2000**

It is also forecast that the business world of tomorrow will require stronger transformational leaders who are able to motivate and inspire a more transient knowledge-based workforce, who, without the stability of long-term careers are unlikely to demonstrate the same level of organisational commitment. The evidence gathered in research to date shows that women score consistently higher on transformational leadership, focusing on motivational and supportive styles. However, many women still opt to leave the world of business for a number of different reasons. There is therefore a strong business imperative for helping women to understand how to be successful and to maintain the option of remaining in the workplace. Retention strategies are therefore as critical as those for attracting high calibre staff in the first place and this is increasingly as applicable to men as it is to women.

'Fathers are rarely happy about being absent from so much of their children's lives either, but at least they have tradition to help them accept it.'[6]

A less buoyant job market may temporarily mask this shift as individuals are faced with fewer choices in the market however the underlying trend remains the same.

Corporate Britain

Britain has the second highest working hours culture in Europe yet both the male and female managers surveyed in the KPMG report voiced dissatisfaction with work/life balance. This

---

6. **"Britain's Top 50 most powerful women," Patience Wheatcroft, Management Today, April 2000**

highlights just one of the many contradictions of the world we operate in today and which men and women find increasingly difficult to manage in a satisfactory manner.

It is interesting to note however that the authors were unable to determine where there were any significant differences according to gender. Why? – there were insufficient women in the sample. It did however provide some more encouraging conclusions.

'Business leaders, it seems, are making working life more effective and, as a result are able to spend less time in the office and more with families and friends. Taking time away from work to relax and take a new perspective on work is beneficial not only to the individual, but also to the company and it seems that this encouraging trend is being driven – in part – by technology, as IT begins to deliver time savings for individuals.'

Recent research conducted by the Graduate Recruitment Company[7] also indicates that tomorrow's managers, the graduates of today, both male and female, are attaching a much higher value to work/life balance than their predecessors. Many have seen parents' health and relationships suffer as a result of work pressures and are simply not prepared to make that sacrifice.

Pearson's recent appointment of Rona Fairhead as Financial Director merited considerable attention from the broadsheets as they became the only organisation in the FTSE 100 to have two female executive directors.

In 2002, it is still a media story when a woman is appointed to a senior, high-profile position in a large organisation,

---

7. **"Graduate Attitudes 2001", The Graduate Recruitment Company**

highlighting that there is still room for change, particularly in the lower echelons of business where the future leaders will emerge. As Management Today[8] put it, 'what really matters are the upcoming numbers in corporate life, the familiar experience, the critical mass. That moment when it's no big thing – precisely because it is so big...'

In the light of these trends and the constantly changing pressures of work and society *'A Bird's Eye View'* offers practical advice for managing those challenges. There is no intent to offer a right way to do things, nor is there only one option to choose. Whilst the interviews highlighted opinions about what makes women successful and where they differ from men it is more about how individuals operate and manage their careers than a gender stereotype.

It is not a question of trying to establish that women make the best leaders because of particular characteristics nor that all women will be successful – the most successful organisations will use the skills of all their employees as effectively as they can. As participants in the Management Today survey points out, 'Gender has nothing to do with ability to manage. It is a case of drive, personality and intelligence' ... 'the best bosses I've had have been male and female – it's not the gender, it's the person.'

The primary aim is to offer women ways in which they can maintain options as they go through, leave and return to their working life so that they feel they are in control and have a choice. Whether they stay at home or choose to return, it is their value set that is important – not what others think they should be doing.

---

8. "The Gender Agenda", Peter York, Management Today, October 1999
9. "Baby Hunger", Sylvia Ann Hewlett, Atlantic Books, 2002

Chapter Two

Vital Statistics

When starting out on the research for this book, the main consideration was how to obtain the most useful output for professional women rather than focusing on statistics as means of proving one theory or another.

Interviews were chosen over questionnaires as the most effective way of gaining candid insights and opinions and were predominantly conducted face to face with a small number being conducted over the telephone. Between them, the senior women interviewed brought experience of a broad range of industries and sectors, spanning PR, technology, media, manufacturing, professional services, consultancy, retail, FMCG, publishing, healthcare and e-commerce. By definition, the fact that they responded indicated an interest in the subject and a desire to help the generations of women coming through behind them.

All the interviews were structured to cover the following areas without being too rigid, allowing each individual to spend the most time talking about the issues she felt most strongly about. Commitment to output the material anonymously meant that the interviews were extremely open and candid.

Career path

This section of the interview was designed to establish the route taken to their current role, how much had been luck, how clear were their short- and long-term goals and what drove the decisions?

? Had they always had high aspirations to run a business and been viewed as high fliers within their organisations?

? Had career moves and decisions felt risky at the time or did they perceive them to be risky in retrospect?

? Did they ever doubt their ability to do the roles they were applying for or being asked to do? If so, had that fear of failure or being 'found out' been something they had learned to deal with over time and if so how?

Organisational environment

We read a great deal about family-friendly and gender-blind organisations and industries and so it was interesting to explore the types of environment in which recognition was given readily for performance and achievements and how significant that recognition had been in terms of building self-confidence and a sense of value.

Women are renowned for being less proactive at promoting themselves and their performance internally than their male counterparts and so we explored whether the organisations that they had moved through were ones in which it was easy to gain recognition for achievements.

? Did they have to learn how to gain that recognition – was it naturally their style and how did they adapt?

? Did this lead to promotion or did they have to push?

? Had they had experience of rapid promotion within an organisation?

? Had this resulted in managing peers or former bosses?

? How did they deal with it?

? How supportive were the organisations they were in – what was the state of organisational readiness for senior women – how did it manifest itself and how did they deal with it?

Many had been the first women at their level and so had some interesting tales to tell.

Values

Here we talked about the motivators for taking roles and judging their personal success together with the importance of the values of an organisation.

? Were personal values always aligned with those of the organisation they were part of and had it mattered?

? Had getting results while maintaining a certain set of values been important to them in their career and had this ever been in conflict with any of the organisations they had been part of?

? How did they reconcile that?

Other issues

The interviews also covered a number of other issues. Support mechanisms both at work and at home were raised as important factors and were ascribed such a degree of importance that they merit a chapter of their own. Chapter 6 examines to what degree the women had had role models, mentors or coaches at critical points in their career, how important they felt this had been to them and whether they now played those roles for other women. It is worth noting that none of the women felt it was possible to sustain a 'Superwoman' role, singlehandedly tackling the combined challenge of work and home.

As career versus motherhood is still a hot topic for debate, and a natural follow-on from the discussion around support mechanisms, we also talked about the delicate balancing of home and work lives, what trade-offs they felt they had had to make and whether or not they had been worth it. More than two-thirds of the women interviewed were mothers. Did they feel they had achieved a satisfactory work/life balance or was this one of the sacrifices they had had to make?

To complement this, we also looked at what sort of mechanisms and approaches they had in place to juggle the many competing priorities, manage stress and talk through issues that were troubling them. Had they had support from other women, partners, family or friends elsewhere that had helped them deal with some of the conflicts and challenges faced in the workplace and/or at home?

Finally the women were invited to give three key pieces of advice they would like to pass on to any professional women reading this, based on their experience over the years and what they know now.

The managers of tomorrow

Additionally, interviews were conducted with a number of female final-year undergraduates, all of whom had had some work experience and some of whom had secured jobs upon graduation. They came from a mix of home, educational and degree backgrounds. However, all had been brought up to be high achievers and carried the weight of the expectation that that will continue when they move into the world of work.

These interviews focused upon their expectations, aspirations and experiences of the workplace. Whilst their experiences were limited, their awareness of some of the challenges ahead mirrored those talked about by the senior businesswomen underscoring the continuing need for sharing those insights.

These interviews focused upon how clear they were about their career choices.

? Who had provided support and advice?

? Had they had any role models they could look to and why had they chosen those particular first jobs?

? Had they always had a clear idea of what they wanted to be longer term and why?

? What were their drivers and how would they define success?

? What did they think would be important to them in choosing future jobs?

? What was important to them in getting their first job?

? What did they think would be important in determining how well they progressed in their careers?

We explored the level of awareness of networking, informal

cultures, relationship building, self-promotion, having a mentor/champion and so on, as influential factors in their career.

On a more personal note, we discussed whether they wanted to combine careers with having a family and how they thought they would be able to manage that.

? Did they see themselves being in a dual career relationship?

? How easy would that be to manage?

? Did they think they would have to make compromises?

Whilst this is a small sample of individuals, they are nonetheless indicative of the generation emerging from the traditional, competitive, academic environments and who are clearly much more streetwise in terms of career choices and far more measured and demanding in their assessment of the options than their predecessors. It is no longer a given that they will move to stereotypical jobs upon graduation and organisations may well need to adapt to their changing attitudes in the long-run rather than merely escalating pay packets to attract them.

Work experience had shown them that, contrary to what they had been told throughout their education, they were not entering a level playing field.

The following chapters have been structured to reflect the key areas that came out of the interviews – career path, self-doubts/self-management, support mechanisms, values, work-life balance and key tips from the top. I hope you find them useful.

Chapter Three

Sense or Sensibility?

Today's young people and undergraduates are encouraged to think about career choices from a very early age. Careers advice starts at school and students are urged to select A levels and degree courses on the basis of their chosen career. Profiles of successful business people in the press back this up with the impression that most have always been very clear about what their career goals were from a very early age. Certainly the undergraduates interviewed for this book were very streetwise about the options open to them and the lifestyle implications of particular types of roles and careers.

A clear plan?

Clear career plans were certainly not the case amongst the women profiled in this report. It is perhaps a reflection of their generation and the job market in which they found themselves that, in all but one of the cases, none of the women we talked to had planned her career path. Indeed, the one individual who had set her sights on becoming CEO of a particular organisation achieved her goal by her mid-thirties and now wonders what opportunities she may have missed along the way. Having a clear focus may have been instrumental in achieving her goal relatively quickly but now that goal has been achieved, what next?

> **'I was over-clear in my twenties about what I wanted to do. Life takes you all over the place. I wanted to be CEO of this organisation. There were lots of staging posts along the way and I knew what was next. Now I'm here I don't know where to go. Maybe I should have gone out and experienced other organisations along the way.'**

Perhaps it is confirmation that talented individuals can be successful and take more career risks than other more ordinary mortals. If you have the capability and drive to make a high value contribution to a business, then you are in a position to make more choices and be more discerning about what suits you as you progress. Whatever the reason, the changing nature of the world of work, the shift to portfolio careers and flexible working mean that even more options will be open to the young professionals of the future. For the senior women interviewed however, whose careers began between fifteen and thirty years ago, the working environment was considerably different and much less flexible.

We asked how they started out in their first jobs, what they knew about the world of work, what their aspirations were at the time and what factors had led them to make subsequent career moves. Not one of the women interviewed had had a burning ambition from an early age. In most cases, their first jobs were taken on the basis that they sounded quite interesting and paid reasonably well, with very little knowledge of what they actually entailed or what the industry was like.

For the majority, subsequent career choices were made upon the basis of intuition, timing, what they would learn, the people they would work with, personal circumstance, and lifestyle. More often than not they were taken opportunistically.

'...there certainly wasn't a grand plan and I have to say that by and large I don't see many people who do have grand plans. Things make sense in retrospect and when they look back there is a certain logic but generally it's about events such as a head-hunter calling you at a particular point – there's no real planned path.'

'I didn't have a career plan and slightly disapprove of them. I tended to look at a few interesting opportunities. People shouldn't be so interested with money and power that they end up doing really boring jobs – they can miss out on really useful pieces of experience along the way which mean that they could do the really top jobs later.'

' I chose a company that had a CEO who was very much in favour of recruiting and retaining women. It was a gut feeling and intuition that it was the right type of organisation for me.'

'I hadn't particularly thought about my career and did whatever seemed right to do at the time and when the opportunity was there. I'm not a great believer in trying to

map out your life. Make sure you are getting exposed to new things, skills and new situations – if you're good, then you will get recognised and there will be demand for you to do the next thing.'

The Saxton and Bamfylde report in 1999[1] underlines our findings showing that successful women were unlikely to retrospectively view their career as having been a campaign.

'What drove them upward was the matter in hand, the enjoyment and the sense of achievement that came from addressing challenges and opportunities. In no case had there been an ambition or strategy of self-advancement for its own sake.'

Jobs for the boys?

Few had been tapped on the shoulder for internal moves. Whilst head-hunters were involved in their more senior external moves, internal moves had generally been achieved through competitive selection processes, an approach strongly supported. One individual commented:

'I am a great advocate for competitive processes whatever the level of the role. Women are often overlooked because they don't have the profile or they don't promote themselves enough. It was hard to get recognition for achievements – it's still a very male culture as most of the management is still very male dominated despite the Chairman being very committed to Equal Opportunities'.

---

1. "Glass Ceilings or Mirrors", Saxton Bamfylde Hever plc, October 1999

Although from the outside these women appear to have taken some risks in terms of changes of career direction, entering male dominated industries and organisations and turning down or giving up jobs to go to Business School, they themselves do not perceive their actions to have been particularly risky. Their decisions were taken because it seemed like the right thing to do at the time. One individual left a well-paid role to join a small start-up in a market about which she knew nothing ...

'... **as it turned out that was a life-changing decision because that business went on to be tremendously successful with a $5 billion market cap over 12 years.**'

'**If you're lucky enough to find work that you enjoy, I think you're really lucky. My driver isn't 'I want that job or its time I moved on' – its more 'I think I could do that better than its done now'. It's more something that grows from within because you realise that you're good at it. I've never had a plan except that if I don't like what I'm doing I'll go and do something else.**'

The measure of success

This characteristic of taking decisions on what they felt they would enjoy or according to gut feeling may, on the face of it, appear to be whimsical in the context of traditional career plans and measures of achievement but can perhaps be explained by exploring a slightly different model of ambition and success. The more commonly accepted model with which we are all familiar is that which is measured by external, quantifiable factors such as status (job title, type of car, where you live, size of team and so on) and is based on performance relative to peers and colleagues (i.e. am I doing better than so and so?). As this model is intrinsically competitive with others, individuals do not really have control over their own level of success – they can control only their own performance not that of those with whom they are comparing themselves. Success or failure depends to some degree on other people doing well or badly. One interviewee cited a former colleague who was constantly dissatisfied because she was always assessing her performance and progress relative to her peer group, a permanently frustrating approach as you can only control your own performance – not that of other people.

The other model is one that more women appear to follow historically – 'let me try and figure out what I want in a holistic way and then I'll work out what the trade-offs are' – and can take a lot of courage, as they need the conviction to move against the accepted notion of success. It may inhibit their progression in a traditional status-measured environment but that's their choice and their own model of success – it's other people using other models of success who would judge that they weren't achieving their potential.

Proponents of this model may say they have achieved because they can manage their job and still collect their child from school. To follow this approach requires a high-level of self-belief to insulate against those who may label this as being 'unsuccessful'.

In the case of the women interviewed, new roles had been taken because they believed in the value of what they were there to do and high personal standards are what drove the exceptional performance. Role changes were often prompted because they no longer felt they were learning or that the organisation could no longer offer them opportunities of interest. Or they felt that the lifestyle demanded by the job meant that their roles as mothers and wives were unrewarding and unsustainable and in that context they no longer felt successful despite results in the business arena. Instead of complaining about the organisation not being family friendly or the demands being unreasonable they took control and actively sought other challenging roles that offered a more flexible approach.

On occasions, they began to look at other people doing jobs and felt they could do that role more effectively. As they rose up the organisation and had visibility of more senior people, they began to consider that they could be successful in executive positions. The fact that early in their careers they did not consider themselves to have the potential to be organisational leaders will be explored in a later chapter.

In only one instance could an individual cite a time when she took a role because of the CV points it would add rather than the job content. She hated the experience. All of the women believed that you could only perform at your best when you are doing a role you enjoy. This became even more critical when they became mothers – the trade-offs are too high to be doing a job you don't enjoy.

A bumpy ride

Careers were not without setbacks or problems. Early redundancies provided valuable lessons and opportunities for a number of those interviewed. Some amongst the women had been accused of being promoted because of personal relationships, others were promoted over their peers who then tried to undermine them. One was told to take elocution lessons to get rid of her accent, another was told she couldn't be promoted because she was a single mum. More menacingly, one individual was warned not to set the benchmark performance so high; in another role she was told she wouldn't last a year. One individual asked whether the fact that she did not have a first class degree would be a problem and was told that the only problem she had was being a woman.

In all cases, the women refused to see these issues as their problem or their issue, and learned to confront the individuals concerned. In most instances, men who were threatened by their level of performance were even less comfortable when asked outright if they had a problem working with or for a woman. The women also ensured that they remained focused on their role so that their level of performance was never questioned and was continuing proof of their capability and contribution to the organisation they were in.

Saxton and Bamfylde's report found that their sample of successful women all had a very high level of education in common. In contrast, whilst all the women interviewed are unquestionably bright and commercially astute, there are no commonalities in background in terms of level of education. Nor are there strong parental role models other than a strong encouragement to do well, whatever they chose to do. Some of the women are graduates – some aren't; some had working mothers – some didn't; but they all have a strong work ethic instilled from an early age, a strong set of personal values and always viewed having a career as an option. This upbringing has also resulted in the fact that the highest pressure for performance in almost all cases came from within.

Setting the standard

In almost all the cases, these women were trailblazers. Often the only woman or the first at their level, they had very few, if any, role models to look to. What they all learned to do was to use the fact that they were women to their advantage – in the more traditional environments they found that senior men did not really know how to treat them or what to expect, so they were able to define their own roles and rules. Although it is telling that some prejudice was encountered, both overt and subtle, they did not let this inhibit their contribution or performance.

'Play to your strengths as a woman – smile, let people be patronising and then surprise them.'

'You have to learn not to react to being patronised. You get desensitised to being patronised but now I notice it a bit more as it's more unusual. It's difficult to never react – every now and again you do.'

When asked whether they would recommend a structured career path, the response was generally cautious on the basis that you can never know all the opportunities that may come your way. The general consensus was to 'never say never'. Whilst they recognised that the world of work has changed to require some planning, their advice was to remain open-minded and wherever possible to leave yourself with more than one option recognising that you might not always get it right first time.

'Be prepared to change and admit it if you made the wrong choice.'

One key emphasis was to ensure that learning was a continual process either through formal courses, management education or by taking on new roles. At more senior levels, taking on non-executive roles provided a breadth of experience that brought a different perspective to their own role and business. It allowed them to learn about how other businesses and sectors operate and to see their skills and contributions from a different perspective.

The way in which career paths were viewed generally reinforced the principle of a model of success based around individual values as opposed to more traditional competitive and status-driven ambitions. For many, career decisions were made more as a result of gut feeling than rational assessment. Decisions were taken on the basis of whether the move felt like the right thing to do rather than a more cynical assessment of the 'CV points' that would be obtained to move them closer to a long-term goal.

> **'Coming here was an emotional choice – I liked the role and it was near where I lived – that can be a very significant factor.'**

One individual turned down a promotion to do an MBA because it felt like the right thing to do at the time. Another was set to leave her career path to retrain – a course of action that was halted by the fact that she found she was pregnant, not by any career motivators.

What appears to have been important to all the women interviewed has been a sense of what they need to learn, an ability to recruit and motivate good people and a sense of a job well done.

> **'What drives me is the opportunity to do what we're doing with the organisation. We have a very unusual opportunity – we have a great culture and that's what keeps me going.'**

Typically they have worked to high standards set by themselves and that has been what has set them apart from the rest. They are driven by a need to believe in what they do and their ability to deliver. Generally they have been regularly put into roles where their comfort zones have been pushed but their determination to learn and to do the job well has carried them through.

Keeping focus

So what do the women put their success down to? The Saxton Bamfylde report highlighted a number of characteristics evident in its sample. One of the key characteristics was the ability to maintain a positive outlook and move forward after encountering setbacks. Their interviewees also felt that the attention to the matter in hand rather than personal status was a useful and advantageous female trait.

During the interviews for *'A Bird's Eye View'*, it became clear that all the women interviewed were very talented and extremely capable. However, the innate intellectual horsepower required to operate in business at their level has also been underpinned by having a strong team, interpersonal and organisational skills.

> **'There's a lot of having the skills in the first place. Being well qualified is half the job whether you're male or female, the other 50% is being able to cope with the job – being able to assert yourself, manage your time, priorities and tasks, having self-discipline, having high standards – its all of those things put into one.'**

In general, the women put their success down to working hard at building relationships, recruiting excellent people on to their teams to fill their own skills and experience gaps and focusing on the job in hand. Strong interpersonal and people management skills were also viewed as being critical if you surround yourself with good people.

An acute self-awareness facilitates recruiting complementary skills into a team where the sum is most definitely greater than its parts.

'I worked very hard at managing team relationships, team building, one-to-one relationships, encouraging openness. I have a lot of people who work for me who are better than me, who have skills and experience that I don't have – you need to be sensitive to that and recognise that – men seem to see that as a threat. That's good for me because we achieve better results. You have to think about handling those people sensitively – delegate to them and recognise their skills and ability, don't over-manage them and give them space. I think your management style evolves over a long period of time.'

'Because my career built slowly, it hasn't been too difficult to change perspective to being more strategic and it has given me the opportunity to reflect.'

Other women profiled in the media hold a similar view. 'Women are less status conscious and will often sacrifice a chance to get to the top for a more interesting and challenging role. They are also less interested in playing silly politics and in the end are more likely to set up their own business.'[1]

This observation is borne out in the reasons given by a number of individuals for moving on and why they may have taken roles that on the surface appeared smaller but in the longer term proved to be a better fit for them.

'I could play the game but I didn't want to. Initially you

---

1. Daily Telegraph Business File, March 9th, 2000

work very hard to fit in and it's only when you grow in confidence that you feel you can be yourself.'

In one case, the move represented a significant downscaling of management responsibilities in the short-term, a move which paid off longer term.

'I had been running a department of forty and joined a department of three. Since then, there has been a huge change in the organisation.'

Career choices, therefore, were on the whole taken opportunistically and driven by a genuine interest in the role and contribution to the business. As the employment market changes and an increasing value is put on leadership and knowledge management skills, organisations will need to pay attention tothe differing motivators of those the need to attract.

Fast-growing companies and sectors are more likely to focus on the talent that they need – in a competitive arena they cannot afford to select by gender or any other prejudice. Other organisations that do not have an immediate imperative to adapt may quickly find themselves at a disadvantage. And it is interesting to note that more and more women are setting out to create their own businesses enabling them to create their own operating environments.

All in all, the evidence gathered here would suggest a flexible approach to career planning, wherever possible keeping options open rather than closing avenues off.

... Key Points ...

- There is no one right way to build your career.

- Focus on what you are good at and what you enjoy.

- Focus on the job in hand – don't let it get personal.

- Use the fact that you are a woman to your advantage if you're in a male-dominated environment – never let it be an obstacle or become an issue that gets in the way.

- Focus on what's important to you not what other people think you should do.

- Trust your intuition.

- Be clear about your vision of success and be true to it.

Chapter Four

'What If I fail?'

Throughout the interviews, one theme came through loud and clear and was particularly surprising in the light of what these women have achieved during their careers and continue to achieve now. Almost without exception, they had questioned their capabilities at various stages of their careers. Clearly they are all talented individuals who set themselves extremely high standards.

However, they are their own fiercest critics. This has resulted in a heightened self-awareness that comes to the fore every time their comfort zones have been tested.

Importantly, this level of self-awareness means that they also recognise this to be a potentially inhibiting trait and one which they see in more of their female than male colleagues.

'Men don't share that sense of doubt – they will look at a job where they can do two thirds and not the other and think they will wing it – women focus on the one third they can't do and assume that means they can't do the job.'

The fear factor

As an independent observer, you would not have any reason to suspect that they doubt themselves in this way. However, their high standards and the desire to do the very best job they can are often counterbalanced by a very powerful fear of failure.

'The female thing about "I'm going to be found out" is often there and I have always had that. I think I'm reasonably self-aware and I know what I'm good at and what I'm not so good at and by and large have tried to focus my career on the things I know I'm good at – 'know thyself' is the advice I would give – don't do things just because you think you should.'

'I went to work for someone who was very clever and competent and I worried that he wanted me there as I wouldn't be competition for him. Did he really want me because he thought I was any good?'

'I did wonder whether I could do things well and whether I would be successful at the early big promotions. I think it's a big issue for women – lack of self-confidence – not enough is done to build women's self-confidence more and you hear a lot of women saying that they can't do things.'

'I do have self-doubts about what I'm capable of – over

time you learn through experience, results and other people that you're good. There's no downside to giving positive feedback as long as it's honest.'

Although rationally there was no reason to doubt their own ability, these feelings often surfaced. If these self-doubts had been allowed to dominate they could have become negative and self-limiting so how had the women learned to harness and manage those doubts so that they became positive drivers?

Not being afraid to ask the stupid question came out time and time again as an important lesson to learn. All too often they had seen other people who were afraid of appearing stupid and had left a meeting without a full understanding, which later came back to haunt them. More often than not, asking the question generated relief from other people who also needed clarification and improved the rapport within the group.

'I've learned that you should say when you don't understand something and, nine times out of ten, you discover that no-one else understood it either.'

That level of self-awareness was therefore used constructively rather than being allowed to inhibit progress. By not being blasé about their ability to excel more thought, effort and resolve is channelled into obtaining the desired result. Focusing on the outcome has driven a pragmatic and results-driven approach. Equally, it means that they genuinely know if they are really getting out of their depth and whether they can manage their way out of the other side.

'I often think 'oh, my god, how I am going to manage this?' You have to learn two things – when to say 'yes, I'm sure we can manage that' and the other is when to say 'I'm

sorry, I don't know the answer to that but I'll go and find it out'. Know when not to bullshit. You have to learn your limitations.'

'After my first day, I thought is this the biggest mistake I ever made? What did I say at interview that made these people think that I can do this?'

One interviewee said she was often apprehensive but had got better at not showing it. She had developed an internal network of people she had known a long time that she could bounce ideas off. As a result, her worry level had gradually changed over the years – now she can tell herself 'you know you're going to get through this – you've done it before'.

'I always question whether I can do a role. I question my judgement and leadership. In all my senior roles, there have been huge lows – I do something right and then come through the low feeling good that something has gone well. I hope I have the self-awareness to know when I have reached my ceiling.'

Understanding the strengths of others

Knowing your limitations and when to ask for help is clearly not the same as being incapable and all the women we interviewed were careful to ensure that when they asked for help they did so confidently so it was seen as a strength rather than an indicator of weakness. In many instances, they discovered that roles or tasks were nowhere near as tough as they had thought once they got stuck in to the job at hand. Breaking the overall objective down in to a number of tasks and a highly developed ability to multitask was often their starting point and provided a way through. Often, their inclination to self-doubt was transformed into feelings of surprise and satisfaction when they succeed.

> **'As it turned out, it wasn't nearly as hard as I thought and I was much better at it than I would have expected. I have a very healthy dose of scepticism around my fundamental capabilities to do what I do.'**

They all recognised the importance of building a strong team who may have higher levels of expertise in some areas – learning to see that as an advantage rather than a threat was a key pointer. An awareness of strengths and limitations and a natural ability to seek out expertise and talent to work with them has played a major part in their ultimate success. Naturally strong team players who are more interested in doing the job well and focusing on the job in hand than politics or status, they set out to create the best teams they can.

> **'How do I cope in those situations? Get my head down ... I have also learned, (because my job is huge and the jobs of the people who work for me are huge and they are all more capable of doing their jobs than I am) to surround myself with very good people.'**

> **'I have always had a very strong fear of failure as a driver – I always believed I was about to be found out ... I know my one real skill is getting results through other people so I build a team full of people that are better than me.'**

> **'Managing a team which has a diversity of styles is critical but exhausting. Play to your strengths and use your team to complement your weaknesses. '**

'I very much believe that men and women complement each other in the workplace as well as in every other aspect of life. I'm not a feminist that would deliberately hire women to increase numbers. I do look at balancing groups because of the skills they bring rather than gender specifically. In my view it's not coincidental that there are so many women in advertising, PR and marketing – it's not just a soft option it's because if you are a total marketer you have to be able to juggle a lot and be good at a good deal of things. Men are much better at being focused on one thing and one thing only. Because of our upbringings, women have rarely been able to do that.'

It would appear that the lack of self-confidence generally applies to a specific task or new role rather than a fundamental lack of belief in their capability. It is perhaps more a fear of not performing to their own high standards rather than those of other people that is typical of this brand of fear of failure. This could explain why only one of the women had had aspirations from an early age to be a CEO – in the main, the others did not automatically consider themselves in that light. They never imagined that one day they would be operating at that level. It is only as they progressed and they saw that roles weren't as difficult as they had thought that they began to see that they could do a better job than the people around them, that they started to entertain the thought of being senior executives.

'I'm not at all ambitious – I never thought that I wanted to be MD. The first time I was made a Director, I was called up for a meeting with my boss and I didn't believe him – I left the office thinking he was joking. My initial response was 'I can't do that – I don't know how to be a director' – he told me I did it all the time. The driver for me is

probably the fact that I don't like the idea of anybody else doing it. I interfere with things if I don't think they are being done well.'

'They promoted me on 1 April so I thought it was a joke.'

'I wouldn't have said before that I was the person to do it but it turned out that it wasn't as hard as I thought it would be.'

One of the more obvious, yet still valuable lessons, which emerged, was not to forget that the people around you also have self-doubts and have their own limitations, so a lack of self-confidence doesn't mean you are wrong. Trusting intuition, doing what felt like the right thing and standing their ground was also high on the list of how they learned and why have they have been successful.

'You acquire these things from experience and sometimes it's just a feeling you have.'

Drawing on prior experience and being certain that they had done the very best they could is a more pragmatic approach which helped certain of the individuals to cope with their doubts and worries.

'Now I have so much experience I don't often think what happens if I can't do this? My way of dealing with pressure is to think, well this is the best that I can do. I can't do any more than this, I have put a lot of time and effort in, I think deeply about things, I take a lot of advice from people, I'm very energetic – if the sum total of this is that I do the wrong thing or I get it wrong, well there's nothing else I can do.'

'I am a late starter. I'm the tortoise rather than the hare and much was probably due to lack of self-confidence. There were no female role models at all. How did I deal with that? Being put into big jobs and having to cope and finding that I could get on top of them and make a success of them and manage the key issues. Once you have done it once, it's easier the next time. Having setbacks along the way and not getting the jobs you want helps you deal with disappointments in the big jobs.'

'I had some awful situations to deal with which were so stressful and difficult to deal with that now I can think that nothing can ever be that bad. If I can do that, I can do anything.'

Proving their worth

Learning how to stand their ground in new environments and taking responsibility for what they were doing whatever the outcome was seen by the women as another tactic for ensuring that they were taken seriously. Establishing a reputation for what they had done rather than managing a perception of what they had done was the most typical response.

'I had to learn how to stand my ground and be assertive – that gives you a core of believing in yourself. Be prepared to stand up and be counted and if you make a mistake you make a mistake. Establish your credibility and deliver – that's all senior people want to know, whether you are going to deliver.'

However, it is no secret that doing the job well is only half the story in most organisations. The other half is about ensuring that other people know the job was well done and managing their profile is not something that came naturally to these women. One or two learned how to actively manage their profiles effectively, the others moved into arenas where their performance was quite clearly defined and measurable such as circulation or sales figures. Or, they moved into organisations where the culture was to recognise contributions and to make individuals feel valued. They all recognised the power and influence of profile within an organisation but preferred a meritocratic model to one where they had to proactively manage their reputations and make sure the right people noticed. In short, a less overtly political environment.

> **'As I progressed, I got skilled at positioning for recognition – I learned from my mentor that perception is reality – it's difficult when you're developing products since if it works, it's due to sales force brilliance – if it flops, it's all my fault. I understood intuitively who to tell to get good news to travel.'**

> **'It has always been easy for people to judge performance – I have never been conscious of having to self-promote and have a horror of it.'**

> **'I get recognition now through the share price, staff morale, grapevine comments on my leadership.'**

> **' I don't think I have ever learned to manage my profile – I don't think I do it now. I can still remember when I first realised that having a reputation was really important – I came from an era where we genuinely believed that it was about merit and that if you were good and did well then you would be promoted. After a while, I realised that you**

only need two or three really senior people to be talking you up and that it didn't matter whether you actually had delivered or not – the myth helped your career.'

One individual also took the view that the efforts spent self-promoting could have a detrimental effect on an organisation.

'I think that's a great weakness for organisations. I don't think I have ever actively gone out to promote my achievements and to network, be known. I have always been more interested in doing a good job at the time – I get more satisfaction from that and in the long run it has paid off because what I have done is based upon solid achievement rather than myth. In the end it does get recognised.'

Picking the right place to work

It's difficult to know whether the women interviewed have performed well despite or because of the environments they were in. However, the evidence suggests that some organisations lend themselves to recognition more than others and the women interviewed placed great store on the culture of the businesses they were working within.

'I think it's easier to quantify your performance in a professional services environment than in a corporate environment.'

Whilst one individual had never suffered from not being given credit herself, she had observed clients assuming that the excellent work done by a woman had been done by someone else. Others had found that their high performance resulted in their being badmouthed. That behaviour was typically as a result of their male colleagues feeling threatened. Despite executive managers being supporters of women in senior roles, that open-minded philosophy had not yet percolated down through the organisation and so day-to-day business with middle managers could be difficult and unpleasant. Happily, many of these organisations have moved on and have become more gender neutral although there are still many examples where this isn't the case. Despite knowing that the issue was about their being a woman, the best response was felt never to make it a gender issue – 'keep it professional – don't ever let it become a corporate issue.'

'I have never been conscious of obstacles having been put in my way. I focus on getting on and doing the job, not the politics – people respond to you in terms of how you position yourself – if you behave defensively because you're a woman then people treat you as if you have a chip on your shoulder.'

'Regard men as your colleagues and friends, not your adversaries, because by and large they are.'

Make yourself known

Networking is another area that was seen to be increasingly important as increased responsibility and visibility. Again this is not something many of them enjoyed doing although they recognised that they were quite good at it. Some felt it to be artificial, others would rather be at home with their family and for yet others, it was simply not the environment they would choose to be in. In the more traditional industries where senior women are few and far between, male colleagues could find it difficult to know what to say or how to behave to the extent where social functions could become awkward.

> **'I'm embarrassed for men at these things as they feel they have to make a special effort to talk to you and include you – I wish there were more women and I had the opportunity to meet more of them.'**

> **'People do often assume that I'm 'the wife' when we go to work dos (it's more disappointing when that comes from a younger woman).'**

> **'I still go to company parties and feel a bit intimidated by it although I appear to be quite confident. I'm not very good at being part of a formal network – I would prefer to go home and see my family.'**

Again, adopting a pragmatic approach helps and whilst it may not be the first choice activity for these women, they understand the value to the business and so undertake it to the best of their ability.

> **'You have to learn to make things useful. I do it for the company, not for me so I see it as part of the job.'**

> **'If I have to do it, I might as well do it well.'**

> **'I lack a business network across industries (it's very good within this industry). I've too much focus on the task in hand to broaden. I did learn to play golf, which helped.'**

There was also a recognition that effective networking was a way in which they could help their teams to be successful.

'I actively network outside the company – I don't use it as much as I should. I have networked the group very heavily. I have to work at networking as I'm very comfortable in my own environment. Functions are often male dominated. I see it as a job and work the floor rather than having chit chat which helps me get through.'

'I don't really know people in the industry and I can be a bit insular. I've learned to manage that as it's a necessary evil – pragmatic is a commonly used adjective to describe me.'

... Key Points ...

- It's good to be self-aware. Use that knowledge to build a team which complements your strengths and weaknesses.

- Everything you do is an advert.

- 'If it's to be, it's up to me'.

- Don't be afraid to ask questions.

- Remember you're not alone in having self-doubts.

- Keep it professional.

- Do what you believe is the right thing to do.

Chapter Five

Tightrope

The 2001 Work-Life Balance week was indicative of the increased coverage of the lack of work-life balance for managers in Britain today and the impact of that in terms of stress at home and at work. With more and more media attention being given to stress in the workplace and the impact on the long-term health of individuals, the balance issue is also now being focused on the implications for business performance. The 1999 Business Leadership Survey by KPMG[1] found that younger leaders were spending less time in the office than their older counterparts, reflecting a new trend in business culture, but Britain still has the second highest working hours in Europe[2].

In interviews, final year undergraduates raised work-life balance as a consideration for career choices and first jobs

---

1. **KPMG Business Leadership Survey 1999**
2. **"Britain towards 2010: the changing business environment", Richard Scase, Economic and Social Research Council, August 1999.**

underlining that shift in expectation. This is further supported by research conducted by the Graduate Recruitment Company[3] which showed that a high proportion of graduates valued work-life balance over and above high salaries. This issue is also highlighted by the Chairman of Employers for Work-Life Balance, who commented:

> *'Work-life balance is not simply about women with children, but something that everyone can embrace, irrespective of age or gender. Interestingly, work-life balance is becoming of increasing importance to younger employees. Businesses need to bear this in mind as today's young people will be tomorrow's managers.'*

Research in recent years has pointed to the significant business benefits achieved by a number of organisations that are starting to fully embrace family friendly policies and other work-life balance initiatives.

> *'... employers who provide childcare referral services for their employees save an estimated £2 for every £1 they spend on the services and reduce costs as a result of reduced sickness absences.'[4]*

In addition to cost savings, a whole range of benefits were reported from improved morale and higher commitment to better results and output. Hewlett Packard reported productivity gains from a compressed working week to enable employees to have weekdays off with the family.[5]

---

3. **Graduate Attitudes 2001, The Graduate Recruitment Company, August 2001**
4. **IES Study, "Who Cares? The business benefits of carer-friendly practices", 1997**
5. **"Business Performance and family-friendly policies", Journal of General Management, Vol 24, No 4. Summer 1999, Shirley Dex and Fiona Scheibl**

For the women interviewed, the work-life balance question raised a number of issues. Not all felt that they had achieved a satisfactory balance although some had learned to better manage the overlap between work and home life. For those with families the challenge of balancing work responsibilities with parenting posed as many emotional as practical questions.

Defining the boundary between work and home

Many of the women interviewed found it difficult to switch off from work and had developed a variety of ways to deal with that. Some had developed their own set of rules to prevent work from permanently encroaching on their home life – some having learned the hard way about the potential for damaging their home life. In all cases they were acutely aware of their ability or inability to switch off and the impact that it had.

'Latterly I have felt very responsible for providing support. Balance is essential and nothing is more important than your family.'

'Weekends are very important. I'm excellent at switching off now but I never used to be able to. I do take work home but I make rules for myself, e.g. two hours on Sunday night. Underneath I'm quite undisciplined so I have to make rules to stop things intruding too much.'

'I haven't really learned to manage switching off. On holidays, I don't give phone numbers and I don't call in. I don't take work home (I would rather come back than take it home) – I now really try and draw the line because I'm bad at switching off. I always take all my holiday (I didn't always do that but that comes with a degree of confidence and nobody notices or thanks you for it if you don't take it).'

'My husband wouldn't say I have a good work/life balance. When I'm on holiday, I call in every day and that's because that's my best way of not worrying – I call my PA to check everything's okay and then I can switch off – if I don't speak to her I can't switch off. I don't take work home regularly – I only take it at weekends if I really haven't had enough time to do it at work. I never work on a Saturday – I do the jobs at home.'

Regrettably a few had learned the hard way about the negative impact that work could and did have upon their personal life.

'At times I've got it wrong. I've learned along the way and there are some mistakes I won't repeat – my personal life is too important. I always go out on a Friday. Saturday is sacrosanct – I don't ever work then. Halfway through Sunday I start to think about work again. Make sure you can manage your life – don't learn the hard way.'

'Work seems to end up running the rest of my life. My relationships are not long, not enduring. Experience has shown I can put lots into love and get nothing out of it – lots in to work and I would make progress.'

Taking a practical and pragmatic view is one technique that has helped some of the women deal with the difficulties of switching off from work and focusing on what is really important to them to keep work issues in perspective and to minimise the impact on their life outside work.

'I think where you live and work are tremendously important – I can work long hours and be home in 10 minutes.'

'I am able to switch off quite easily unless it's a real crisis and then I don't sleep. I've learned over the years to rationalise things and also that the first 24 hours are always the worst – after that, things don't ever look quite so bad.'

'Think about what's important to you so that you can see when it's off-track and manage it. I work to live. I keep a horse to maintain an outside interest. I'm disciplined about taking days off and holidays. Try and keep a pragmatic outlook – what's the worst thing that can happen? That helps to stop me worrying.'

'I'm very blessed. I have a husband who has a good job and so I don't have to work if it all goes horribly wrong and I recognise that. That makes it easier to switch off.'

Going home to partners and/or family often helped to put work into perspective, refocusing on the most important people in their lives. Ensuring that those relationships were given enough time and attention was therefore seen as critical.

'Make time to go away together with your partner on your own – that balance is really important.'

'The kids help me to switch off.'

'The way I work out stress is by thinking things through, seeing what I've learned and working out if there's anything I need to do to fix the problem. If I don't talk about it and work it through then I don't get rid of it. Playing with the kids puts everything in perspective. I try not to take work home but I do let off steam with my husband because now I'm in a job where if things aren't right, it's up to me to fix it.'

The business environment

The variety of industries within which these women work highlights the importance of the business culture and environment. Some had deliberately chosen their employer or profession on the basis that it was more flexible and encouraged that balance for all employees. Others found that their working environment inhibited their ability to have a fruitful life outside work. Roles in organisations which allowed autonomy and flexibility for all employees were the most attractive for obvious reasons and by and large were representative of the businesses the women had chosen.

> 'This is a pretty family-friendly organisation and it's the norm for everyone male and female to go to sports days, carol services etc – it's expected of people to do that.'

> 'Many people join us for the balance. Anything where you are a sole trader, e.g. you have a client-base and you're not totally interdependent with a team, you have much more control and flexibility. I have much more control. That's why you see a huge number of women setting up their own businesses as they can set their own rules – often they work harder but they work differently.'

> 'There are other jobs which pay more, there are others which would give more work/life balance and some that offer even more fascinating content but very few that offer all three so well. Given those three things are reasonably important to me, then I have ended up with a great job that I have been able to shape.'

Professional services were seen by some as an environment

which was more suited to flexible working arrangements although this was a matter for debate and it would seem more likely that the individual organisation rather than the sector itself is the biggest factor.

'It's difficult to enable part-time work as clients don't like it if you're not available the whole time – you don't get family-friendly clients and they're paying a lot of money for what you do. I don't know what the solution is. I'm sure there are also a lot of men that would like more flexibility.'

'I never dreamed of coming back part-time – I don't know why as now it seems like a sensible thing to do. People's priorities are different now. Companies are now starting to do quite radical things to poach staff. I think people can be tougher with clients as they have the same issues internally and they are interested in long-term partnerships rather than supplier type relationships. We're very supportive of the career break/part-time options – I don't think that that's common across the industry.'

Within the job market in general, a similar change has been observed in candidates, male and female, across all industries with one of our interviewees commenting:

'There has been a shift in the roles candidates will consider – there's a real focus on family and the working hours.'

Additionally, some of the women had observed a trend for young graduates to be more demanding about work/life balance and for more and more individuals to opt for self-employment as a means of creating a work environment to suit their needs.

'Young grads have a very different view from when I

graduated (they're less likely to take work home, they're prepared to work hard but have their parameters – they want to have a life). There are more people resigning to get out of the industry and take control in their late 20s than ever before.'

'There are more people exploring freelance options etc. That became an option when the recession happened and people have discovered that it's quite an attractive option. There is more of a tendency to take risks. People don't care so much if they make a mistake. People are more portfolio focused and recognise that they will do many different things.'

Again these observations are supported by the findings of the Graduate Recruitment Company with a high percentage of graduates stating that their long-term aim is for self-employment or portfolio employment as opposed to climbing the corporate ladder.

The Foresight report[6] also predicts that over the next decade, long-term careers and employment in a small number of large corporations are likely to decline as employees are forced to be more adaptive, shifting between companies with greater frequency as well as embarking upon periods of self-employment.

People's working lives will be more varied but shorter. The report concludes that as a result employees will have very different psychological expectations.

Most employees will consider their organisational commitments to be temporary. They will have few expectations

---

6. **"Britain towards 2010: the changing business environment", Richard Scase, Economic and Social Research Council, August 1999.**

of long-term careers and will tend to regard employment contracts as essentially short-term negotiated arrangements. All of this should enable employees, male and female, to develop less traditional career paths with breaks or varied commitments to suit their lifestyle and aspirations at different stages of their careers.

In an increasingly competitive business environment, retention of key employees should therefore be high on the agenda for organisations if this is indeed a reflection of the new generation of managers being recruited. Some organisations have already found this to be the case.

'Retention rate improvements were also noted after the introduction of family-friendly policies at the Midland Bank and Glaxo. Glaxo's introduction of flexible work, and childcare services which were self financing, saw the return rate for employees after maternity leave increase from 40 to 97 percent.'[7]

Such issues and policies were generally recognised by the women interviewed as an issue for them as employers as well as employees.

'Before I met my husband, I would always work Christmas hols and never take my full annual leave entitlement – I got my emotional security from work. People get very silly about the long hours ethic. The industry needs to adopt more home and flexi-working arrangements to accommodate people. Fewer and fewer people are on staff contracts, there

---

7. IRS Employment Trends 632, May 1997

are no jobs for life, there's more portfolio working, therefore working arrangements have to be in line with those changes.'

'I never used to think about it but I do now. I can see other people with the same issues. You see work-life balance as a really big issue in the States. The organisation needs to try and get ahead on this for both men and women (not just those with children).'

'If you can offer flexibility as an employer it generates loyalty and you get better value out of people so it also makes business sense.'

'The Women in Management program at London Business School was very helpful – it made me face some of the underlying and implicit issues such as managing dual careers and organisational environment.'

If these issues and aspirations really are becoming more critical in career choices, then there is a real business imperative to adopt more flexible working practices if organisations are to attract and retain key talent.

Dual careers

The majority of women interviewed were also juggling the demands of parenting and being a partner. The increase of dual careers has on the one hand made it easier for women to be accepted as working mothers but has on the other introduced practical difficulties where both partners have demanding jobs.

Some environments were felt to be more conducive than others to accommodate dual careers and work-life balance and this raises another important issue for organisations wishing to attract and retain good people. This seems only likely to increase as an issue. In the Graduate Recruitment Company's survey, some 98% of the respondents with partners anticipated having dual careers, highlighting the need for organisations to be aware of the conflicting demands being placed upon their employees both male and female. Managing the challenge of dual careers was recognised by all the women as an issue for either themselves or women around them.

'Serious dual careers are incredibly difficult to manage – the advantage of professional services is that once you're a partner you carry on doing the same thing and you're not fighting for the next step.'

'The women I see struggling with dual careers are those where the husband doesn't share – sometimes because he can't as the job takes him away five nights a week and so on. The difficult thing as I see it is that in many instances women can succeed if they are prepared to play by the boys' rules but that's really difficult if you're a mother – trying to work all hours doesn't work. There aren't that many women who want to do that (it's a mug's game). There are many more men who want that balance too.'

'This is a single woman's job.'

Becoming mothers raised issues for all the women concerned. The practicalities of childcare, dual careers, feelings of guilt, not wanting to let people down in the workplace are all common themes expressed.

Whilst the interviewees recognised that there was still a long way to go to help women accommodate the dual role of parent and professional, there was also a recognition that the changes in the job market may prove to be an advantage.

'The crunch point is when you have your children. Companies are recognising the need to attract women. I think the other thing that will work in women's favour is that the job-for-life path has disappeared anyway and by and large, careers have become much more fractured – people move around, take time out – that will work in women's favour as there won't be the perfect pattern anymore.'

'I haven't seen the difficulties of being a woman other than the work/life balance issues. Money helps (you need to be able to pay for excellent childcare), a fantastic husband helps, an understanding organisation helps – I earn enough to be able to have wonderful childcare and we've had the same nanny for the last seven years.'

'It has to be very much about 'us' to manage dual careers and household. It doesn't get easier with time but it becomes more manageable. Partners have to make themselves equally available to resolve any issues – it's a parent issue not a mother issue.'

'Most of the time we have had dual careers. Three and half years ago when I came here, my husband retired. The kids know that we're unusual in that my husband's retired and I'm the breadwinner. Some of their friends' mums work, some don't.'

One individual felt that combining both work and motherhood was not something she would be able to do and so made the decision not to have children.

'I see childcare and the work/guilt thing as a big issue for women – I decided not to have children.'

Sadly, this view is underlined in a report that found that one quarter of women managers had sacrificed having a family because of their career, as against one in ten male managers. The publication of Sylvia Ann Hewlett's *'Baby Hunger'* has made the current choices appear even starker. With 40% of the women over 40 she surveyed being childless yet only 14% saying they did not want a family, the evidence from the USA is that the trade-offs for ambitious women are enormous.[8]

Other women have become more demanding in terms of enabling themselves to juggle the demands of work and home and over time found ways of accommodating both.

'My children are the most important things in my life. I've had to demand some compromises – one morning a week I took my daughter to school, one afternoon a week I would leave early to collect her. I'm always to be interrupted if my children call me at work. Children and dual careers mean less focus on the relationship which we're now learning to do again.'

'It's important to have good back-up for when things don't go according to plan. The demands don't lessen but you can get better at the planning and structuring.'

Where dual careers were successful, talking through all the implications with their partner and taking a practical approach was seen as critical on an ongoing basis. The aspirations, needs

---

8. **"The Price of Success - Beyond the Great Work-life Debate",**
Ceridian Performance Partners and Management Today, 1999.

and frustrations of all parties involved are likely to change over time and this needs to be taken into account to ensure that neither party becomes unhappy with their role in the relationship.

> **'To manage dual careers you have to be utterly practical. You have to talk through what it means to be earning different amounts of money up front so it isn't allowed to become an issue. Will it matter who's earning more? Recognise that this may change over time.'**

> **'When push came to shove, it was an easy economic decision. My husband has been unusually laid back about it.'**

> **'It's hard to talk about some of the issues up front – running households and kids is very reactive. You have to make sure that the communication channels are open and that you always invest in taking the time to talk to your partner and see how you are doing – are you both getting what you need?'**

The difficulties of maintaining personal relationships, dual careers and delivering on a professional level were evident from some interviews.

> **'The organisation is the type which expects to be able to call you on holiday/at home etc. My personal needs have changed. I need to be looked after and taken care of and my emotional demands responded to. I need a 'wife' at home to do that.'**

> **'I couldn't have a family. I know that I would want to give up work if I had children and I can't bring myself to do that. There are no women role models in the industry.'**

'My trade-offs have been a lack of personal life and privacy. I'm now trying to develop a network outside work. I'm too dependent on the organisation.'

Seniority

Whilst all of the women interviewed felt that more flexibility should be offered to employees both male and female to accommodate the demands of work and parenthood, they also recognised that in the current business environment this was easier to do at a more senior level. Once they had reached a position where they could control the workload, were confident in their value to the organisation and could afford excellent childcare, then managing their work-life balance became a more realistic option.

'Now I'm in control. I got to my level quite quickly and then had my kids and then relative seniority meant I had more control. It's really hard when you get stuck in the middle – you've progressed reasonably well but don't have enough control.'

Whilst the women recognised that work-life balance was easier to achieve as they became more senior due to the increased control over the business, they also recognised the responsibility which that seniority brings and the additional pressures that that puts upon the balance question.

'It's not a job which concerns just you – you're talking about employees whose livelihoods you are responsible for and that's not something you can take or not take as you choose.'

'I get paid a lot of money not to have balance. I do have some techniques to offset that – I take all my holiday, I plan them a long time in advance and I take them all – I have two children and a husband and they have to know that they get time with you on their own (although I am always contactable).'

'There's no balance. That's the trade-off you make when you take a job as CEO – you can't say to a Board that you won't do it unless you have a balance. That's my choice and I don't have to do it. I could have decided that that was not for me.'

The guilt thing

Despite the fact that the women with children shared the childcare with partners and generally had excellent childcare arrangements, there was still, to a certain extent, a question of guilt.

'You have to have the confidence to be yourself and do what you want to do, know what you're good at and what you're not good at. I have worked really hard at making life consistent for the children and emotional blackmail from them is very rare. What they don't really like is change and they need to know exactly what is happening. Guilt can be hugely destructive – you need to focus on enjoying the time you spend with your children – don't poison it.'

'You always feel guilty about the children. My mother worked and I didn't feel any sense of loss. Whatever the level, it's difficult to work and be a mum because even though husbands can help, you somehow end up carrying the responsibility.'

'I'm the main breadwinner which focuses the mind and helps as you don't have the difficult decision to make about working.'

'The things that have totally gone are the personal pleasures for me. I'm very focused on my kids but I don't think I give them enough normal time (e.g. picking them up from school). On the other hand, when we have time, it's really good and we always do things. I increasingly think it's important to have nothing time for you but I don't have it.'

In some cases, the responsibility for childcare had shifted over time. In one instance, the interviewee had been working three days a week, then, once promoted, she returned full-time with the support of a nanny and when the family relocated for her job, her husband retired.

'I have a good relationship with my kids and they have always known that I work – it's good that they think that I work too much as that means they care and my husband is at home full-time. Kids are brutally honest but they are also like a sponge and whatever you give them they will always want more.'

'I haven't had as much access to my kids from a selfish point of view but I don't think that that has short-changed them. Their outlook on the world in terms of their expectations is really to be open-minded. I am definitely unusual in the level of seniority but I'm not sure my kids differentiate between me and other people whose mums work. What they don't have are friends whose dads don't work.'

Flexibility goes both ways

With the recognition that the world of work has changed so that employment arrangements are more flexible for employers, has come the understanding that this flexibility needs to work both ways so that employees can accommodate different working patterns and still feel valued. Having experienced the issues of juggling career and motherhood, the women interviewed were also very conscious of the impact on the people around them and the knock-on effect of their wanting to work more flexibly. Sensitivity to that was seen as being key to being able to manage a successful work-life balance.

> **'You have to realise that it's disruptive for the people around you at work.'**

> **'I worked very hard to make my part-time schedule not impact on those who had full-time schedules. I made my home life very flexible and worked five days when needed – I tried never to say, 'I don't work Mondays'**

> **'When I had my last child, I was MD – I was never out of the job effectively although they make jokes about it now. I delegated stuff but I kept in touch and maintained signing authority etc, and had to make sure the job got done. You have to negotiate with your employer about what you're going to do.'**

> **'You need two-way flexibility to manage things conveniently – technology has made this much easier. However, women need to understand that if they opt for three days in the office and two days at home when they become mums, they are labelled Mums. It can also breed a**

lot of resentment if they start to leave at 5.30pm regularly when the job requires a late night as other people then have to pick up the workload.'

'I've been careful not to become defined by my role as a working mother. Everyone has the right to work reasonable hours. There's a big cultural problem about long hours. I should be acting as a role model and making it okay for other people. You don't have to be a mother to legitimise the desire to work part-time, work from home one day a week, work reasonable hours. That will become increasingly important.'

'There has to be two-way flexibility – you can have a core of knowing what you want to do and you should try and manage that without making it other people's responsibility to manage it. People don't need to know what your model is – they just need to know how they get what they need. It does help to be a good planner and have well-organised people around you. Other people's bad planning can sometimes cause problems. You have to recognise that there are responsibilities to the job. In more junior roles and more rigid hierarchies, then it can be more difficult for you to manage that. Now I can feel confident enough to say 'no' to doing evening presentations but I don't feel I have to explain why.'

Advances in technology have obviously helped with a more flexible working pattern. However all the comments about the boundaries between work and home become even more pertinent to ensure that the home does not simply become an extension of the office with work becoming all-consuming.

'Home working has helped so that you can still be in contact. You have to recognise the reality that the business still has to be run.'

The 2001 Work-Life Balance week served to highlight the business benefits of allowing employees more flexible working arrangements, whatever their gender. In the short term however, it's likely that it is women who will benefit the most.

In 2002, most family-friendly options are generally seen as being open to women only, indicating that there are still social and cultural changes that still need to take place to allow men and women to truly share the same work-life opportunities if they wish. The issues are as real for men as they are for women although the dynamics are different.

With 79% of the KPMG survey respondents reporting an adverse impact of work on their relationship with their spouse/partner and 86% an adverse impact on their relationship with their children, the implications for society, family structures and business are wide-ranging.

Whilst this is becoming a more high profile issue, many organisations are only now starting to look at their arrangements (if at all) and the work-life balance issue is one which individual women are likely to have to find their own solution to for some time to come.

... Key Points ...

- Make your own rules and stick to them.

- Talk to your partner and work out how best to manage dual careers if that's what you want.

- Look at the work ethic and culture of the organisation when you join. Be clear about the role, responsibilities and expectations before you accept – remember you have a choice.

- Be sensitive to the impact you may have on family, friends, clients, customers and colleagues.

- Flexibility has to work both ways.

- Remember you may be a role model for others – show them it's good to have that balance.

- Don't let guilt poison the time you spend with your children.

Chapter Six

Helping Hands

One of the common factors to which the women attributed their success was having effective support mechanisms. The support varied from having help on a practical level to having an emotional outlet when things got tough. Importantly they recognised that it was an impossible task to try and do everything themselves. As one interviewee put it:

'Do you believe in the Superwomen claims? No. There are only so many hours in the day.'

Balancing a demanding job with being a partner and parent was not viewed as something that could be achieved without help of some kind. Despite all the high profile career women who are described as Superwomen who do it all, the reality is that when you probe a little deeper, they all have help on one level or another. Nicola Horlick's frank account of her experiences that propelled her into the public eye shows that without family support, a nanny and an understanding organisation and colleagues, maintaining her career progression and family life would have been exceptionally difficult.[1] Having friends and confidantes to talk to, especially in times of crisis, was highlighted over and over again during the interviews.

> **'It's important to have people you can compare notes with and talk to and relate to unless you're a real loner – you need people to talk to who aren't directly impacted by what you're talking about – a shoulder to moan to.'**

> **'I could not have done this without my husband – you must choose your mate very carefully – you cannot do this if your husband does not support you. We share everything – he can cook Sunday lunch just as well as I can and he has never had a problem with any of that.'**

> **'I could not have done this without him – I can't imagine what it would be like to be a single mother.'**

> **'Throughout my career, there have been a number of close friends – mentors who have helped me through different issues.'**

Professional sounding boards

On a professional level, most women had clearly identified sources of advice and counsel. In the majority of cases, these women were treading where no women had gone before. The

---

1. **"Can you have it all? How to succeed in a Man's world", Nicola Horlick, Macmillan, 1997**

belief that they could successfully make the next step came not only from themselves but in most cases from another party, be that a boss, a mentor or family. They are remarkable therefore not only for their achievements but for daring to aspire to be something for which there was no precedent. Despite the boldness of what they have accomplished, their belief in their ability to succeed had to be, in most cases, bolstered by others.

'My self-belief has come from my husband, my boss and experience of having done things well over time.'

As discussed in Chapter Four, the level of self-awareness meant that these women knew when to seek advice or input from elsewhere and they were very clear about who they went to for particular types of advice. For some it had been the same person throughout their career and for others it had changed with role, seniority and organisation. The support was not just related to the realities of getting the job done but also to educate them in terms of how the next layer of management operated, how to get allies and how to make themselves known. As proven performers in their roles, these allies were powerful supporters when it came to breaking through the next barrier or setting new precedents.

Mentors and sounding boards within the business environment were a recurrent theme throughout. Having someone objective with whom they could test ideas and approaches and reaffirm their confidence was an important factor for most of the women interviewed in one way or another.

'I've always had a great mentor. He likes the reflected glory but it's also very helpful that he is very successful in his own right.'

'I've never had any female role models but my mentor has always been very good and I couldn't have done it without him and my husband.'

'When I was made MD, I realised how much support I gave to the previous MD – he always used to come in and talk to me first thing every morning and I could sense whether things were going well or not and would ask him. Then he would talk about it. I have been here a year and no one has asked me whether I was alright (the other directors are male and I don't think it has ever occurred to them).'

'My current boss has provided continuity – he's been a boss more than a mentor but he is brilliant, a visionary – we have complimentary roles – he dreams it up and I make it happen. He is someone I can go to with business problems.'

'I now have a Business coach. The Chairman has been a strong influence – I've gained advice and wisdom and have watched and learned how to evaluate and manage particular situations.'

'I had a very strong mentor from whom I learned to have the courage of conviction and I benefited from his network. He wasn't afraid of anything or anybody and I admired him for what he achieved.'

In rare cases, a female role model also provided useful guidance and insights.

'I had a female CEO. There were lots of women in the business but no women running businesses. It's still mainly men now even though the vast majority underneath are women. I got seconded to her and stayed with her for nine months. She had real vision. She took time for other people (which I don't think I do enough). I still use her as a sounding board.'

'My Mother always worked and ran her own businesses. In my experience, successful women have all had very strong women (good and bad) in their childhoods.'

In other instances, that professional sounding board role was played out by partners or friends.

'I have successful friends in business which is very useful. When my father died, I lost my mentor and guru.'

'I talk to my husband who is a good sounding board – he's quite intuitive and can see his way through problems. I belong to one or two professional organisations. I have lots of sources of advice in the organisation.'

'I always talk to my husband about work and also about his business. He's very clever and perceptive and comes up with good ideas. He's not in corporate life and has always worked for himself and is very successful in his own right. He takes the mickey out of corporate life. It's a good leveller.'

'My husband is the most important thing in my life – we've been together twenty years. It's important to have him as a friend and we keep each other grounded.'

Women like me

Having like-minded women to talk to was also seen as important and something that was wished for by those who didn't have it. Whilst support could be given from male colleagues, there is something subtly different about talking to other women juggling work and life and who have the same issues and perspective.

> **'Men don't share personal feelings with each other. Women can benefit from talking – consequently we're better at recognising the needs of other people. My Mother was a very strong influence – positively early on and then less so as she grew older. She was my first boss.'**

> **'My friends are a mixed bag – some haven't returned to work at all, some work part-time and some work full-time. I think I totally miss out on support mechanisms like school-runs etc. My friends are from work or from school, uni, MBA.'**

As most felt that at one point or another they were very much operating in a man's world, they valued the opportunity to have people they could really identify with on a personal level to share concerns, frustrations and provide morale and emotional support.

> **'It's important to have other women in similar positions so that your family and children have other people to identify with. I don't want my kids to be the only ones with a working Mum.'**

> **'It's good to have other female friends in the same**

situation – it helps you reaffirm that what you're doing is right. You can also reflect on what you see happening to them.'

'I've got a very close-knit group of friends to let off steam with. I've a number of close friends who were formerly in the same business. Friendship is very, very important for sanity.'

'I have always had support from family and friends. There's a close group of six of us from University – four of us are still working and, at one point, four of us were the major breadwinners.'

'All my friends are professional women – mainly ex-clients. We provide positive support for each other as a matter of course, 'well done' etc.'

This last comment also reflects the need for recognition, partially tied to the lack of self-belief discussed earlier, and a need to have it reinforced that their contributions are of value. Again, this comes back to a model of success founded on values rather than the more traditional status-conscious measures of achievement.

Given that many of these women were trailblazers, several did not have other female friends or colleagues to turn to. For those without other women to talk to, sitting at the top of the organisation could be very lonely.

'I have quite a broad network of friends and family, quite a lot of whom are men – there weren't that many women around then – sometimes I relate to the men more easily than some of the women. I use the extended family – we're all very close and you know you can call upon each other.'

'Unfortunately, I don't have very many female friends who work. I have two who both work for our PR Company – I'm just starting to socialise with them and I really look forward to that. We have a lot of long-standing friends but no women who I have a lot in common with on a day-to-day basis and they don't have a clue about what my life is like. We're very close but there is something missing.'

'It would really be nice to have female friends who are in similar situations.'

Being a role model for others

As individuals who had lacked role models themselves, the women were very conscious of the fact that as trailblazers they were setting the precedent for women behind them and were being viewed as role models themselves. Whilst feeling that they could help and had advice and support to offer, this also brought an additional pressure to succeed so as not to let those women down.

'It was difficult to come back from maternity leave as I came back after really early – I had just been given a really big promotion to an operational job at a level that no woman had had before. I was very conscious that I was very visible and the most important thing you can do as a role model for other women is to not fail. I feel that it's an additional pressure that men don't have to even think about. As there are so few women, it's really important that they are seen to do well.'

Now leading businesses themselves, these women are being asked for guidance and advice as there are few other sources for younger women to turn to.

'It's important to share experiences with other women as I still see women finding it difficult to break through.'

'Women with practical issues such as changing hours to accommodate taking their children to and from school come and talk to me. People come less to talk about planning forward and more about more emotive issues.'

Choosing the right partner

The support of a partner was seen as being vital in being able to manage home and work demands and it was also recognised that this needed to be acknowledged publicly – most of all to the partner in question.

'He's very placid and not macho – however he does want recognition for the support he gives. The decision to work was taken together and that has always been the way since we met. I still feel emotionally that I'm responsible for things like taking the children to the doctor etc, but he points out that he's perfectly capable of doing those things – maybe it's because they're girls.'

'Having a partner who is flexible and genuinely participating in sharing the home responsibilities and best of all, less committed to his work than I am to mine, is a big factor.'

'My partner is very supportive. He's not really ambitious himself so he's quite content with his role and being

supportive. I used to push him and try and impose my model on him.'

Friends and family

Outside the work environment, support was also drawn upon to meet the emotional and moral support needs and frustrations. As we have already seen, husbands play a critical role but support is also needed from other quarters. Close family and close friends were commonly part of the equation to keep things in perspective and not to let work become all-consuming.

> **'My parents are supportive although my mother does slightly undermine me with implied criticisms such as 'don't work too hard' but they understand that I would be bored at home. She has never voiced any disapproval about my going back to work. She recognised that it wouldn't have suited me to stay at home and she thinks the children are great so that reflects on me okay.'**

> **'I've always felt supported by my family – never judged or criticised.   You need a supportive husband who understands you're not going to take a traditional role and understands what that means in reality – shared responsibility for domestic life and kids etc.'**

> **'My parents are supportive but a little bemused. Now I have children, they are quietly tolerant.'**

On a more practical level, almost all the women had had childcare support and help with the housework. Most had found that nannies were the only workable option for satisfactory childcare providing the children with consistent quality care that could more flexibly accommodate the work demands of a senior executive.

> 'We always had a nanny because I was 33 and I could afford it by then. I never considered anything other than a nanny. I have never had a lot of stamina and so had to have the support and the job meant I needed that flexibility. All of my friends had nannies and so I checked it out with them. You need nannies and cleaning ladies.'

> 'If you have a big job then nannies are the only solution unless you have family to help.'

> 'We've just taken on a nanny/housekeeper instead of just a nanny and that has been a huge help.'

> 'Fortunately my economic situation has meant that I have never had to make tough decisions. I have always been able to hire full-time nannies and housekeepers and whatever has been needed to support my husband.'

> 'He's an old-fashioned man – he doesn't do a thing at home. So I have always had help at home and am fortunate to have always been in the position to have that.'

This they recognise is an advantage brought about by the financial security and income that comes with the level of role that they hold. Childcare is viewed as a much tougher issue for younger women still making their way up through the hierarchy who perhaps can't afford the services of a nanny. Some choose to stay at home because they want to, others simply can't afford the childcare.

> 'There aren't many women here who come back, often

because they're younger and so aren't earning enough to make it worthwhile and their husbands are also often earning much higher salaries and they also like being at home.'

... Key Points ...

- Recognise you can't do everything by yourself.

- Make time for your partner, friends and family.

- Maintain relationships with mentors – know who is a reliable sounding board.

- Find other like-minded women with whom you can share experiences.

- Be prepared to ask for and, when necessary, pay for practical help and make the most of it.

- Don't ask too much of yourself – the Superwomen status is not sustainable and something will give if you're not realistic.

Chapter Seven

True Colours

As we saw in Chapter Three, career choices and decisions were not, in general, made on the basis of status or a desire for material success. Typically, a more subtle model of ambition and measure of achievement was applicable – one in which a feeling of doing something worthwhile, benefiting others and adding value was of most importance. Doing the job well rather than getting on was the motivator and progress was therefore almost a by-product rather than a planned outcome. A high value was placed by the interviewees upon their home lives and their relationships with friends, family and children. If they were going to compromise those in any way, then they genuinely had to feel that they were making a difference in their job role and doing it well.

'I'm driven by a passionate belief in what we stand for. I've only done one role that I didn't want to do. I did it because it

would be good for me and I hated the three years I spent doing it. It was very high profile but I didn't enjoy it and I would not do that again. Not only do I enjoy my job now, I can't believe that I am so privileged to have the job I have always wanted.'

'The key point for me is that although I'm very committed to the company I work for, my responsibilities are to here and to doing a great job so it doesn't feel like I'm committed to my career as such – that feels self-serving and all about progression; Me-focused rather than focused on role and responsibilities. I've never thought about a career as a planned entity but as an outcome – all I'm after is a rewarding series of jobs each of which is more responsible and better paid than the last and which I throw myself into no holds barred.'

Doing their best

A common value was that of doing the job well. Although most had never set out to be running organisations, they had gradually worked their way through realising that they could do the next level of job and were almost surprised to have ended up at the top of the organisation rather than it being the fruition of a successful campaign. As we noted earlier, whilst there may not have been any commonality in educational background, they had all been brought up in environments where, by and large, doing their best was what counted.

'I have a really engrained work ethic from my family background and that has been more useful than any formal qualification. I don't have a lot of sympathy with work-shy people or those who aren't working hard.'

'If there's something I want, then I like to be able to get it and do it well.'

'I place a high value on working and grafting.'

This tactic also seems to have been adopted, at least in part, to counter the inclination to doubt in their ability to be successful, and was adopted from an early age. If they genuinely felt that they had done their best, then they could rest easy in the knowledge that they had given things their best shot.

A belief in doing the right thing, doing something of value, was a primary motivator and one that these women have found to be tremendously rewarding as they became more senior and were able to have a broader influence and impact.

'Women tend to think more about the intrinsic nature of the job they're doing rather than the relativities with other people. I've turned roles down despite the money and so on being fantastic. This job has a very wide range of interest and that's what keeps me.'

'It's fantastic doing this sort of job – I would probably have tried harder to be a CEO if I had known that this was what it was going to be like. It's tremendously rewarding to be able to do the things you believe in, in the way you want to do them. You can implement things you have always believed in and you can implement them big time.'

'I get a big kick out of seeing the service excellently delivered. I go and sit with the people in the call centres and get the instant feedback. Once a week I spend a day in the business. It is quite inspiring to think that we are doing something worthwhile.'

A focus on people

Chapter Four illustrated that, generally speaking, these women made sure to surround themselves with excellent people to complement their own strengths and weaknesses. It was no surprise therefore, to find that high on their list of typical values was the desire to help other people to perform to their best and to enable the business and their teams to grow.

> 'I like to encourage people to perform better (and I think women are more prepared to tell people and help them). I think we empathise better. If someone comes to me with a problem then that becomes my problem as ultimately they're my responsibility. I take it personally if someone fails in a role as that means I got the appointment wrong – it's the nurturing side of us.'

> 'We make a huge effort in terms of communicating with employees and I get a tremendous kick out of the fact that the results improve and you can use that to motivate your managers and directors – it is transformational leadership. That's what gets me out of bed in the morning.'

> 'Making the company successful is more important to me than the people who work here because that's what I'm paid for. If I can't meet their expectations, then there's no future for any us. To facilitate that, I know the importance of the people who work here – they are our number one resource and are all treated with the same fairness and I do take their livelihoods seriously.'

> 'I have high expectations but believe you have to give people the chance to get better.'

The high level of self-awareness was again in evidence here with a great deal of clarity around their personal styles and how their values impacted on the people around them.

> 'I'm very aware of the people implications of decisions. I feel my leadership style is strong – I don't suffer fools gladly. I dislike good news cultures – I tell it how it is. I dislike self-promotion – let the results speak for themselves. It's important to me to be promoted from within – it demonstrates I have been recognised within the organisation. Be true to yourself and understand what that means.'

> 'I'm quite self-aware and try to consider the impact of my behaviour on others. I know that I'm irritable if people don't catch on as fast as me. You need a really good team around you who understand you and your behaviour.'

Organisational culture

Choosing the right sort of organisation was again a consistent theme with a fit between corporate and personal values necessary to promote a fulfilling work environment. This is particularly important as values and culture form the informal organisation around how things actually get done as opposed to the stated way of operating. It has been argued that this informal organisation forms one of the biggest obstacles to women succeeding in traditionally male dominated environments.

In a competitive environment, aligning organisational and personal values was recognised as not always being a straightforward thing to achieve. However it remained a central part of determining whether the women joined, stayed with or left organisations.

> **'The important thing is that you have to live corporate values – e.g. innovation through the company isn't something you say, it's something you live. What's most important to me is myself and my family. My husband thinks it's my job, which is extraordinary, because it isn't. Anyone who says their job comes first is either a complete idiot or not telling the truth.'**

> **'When I was approached for two or three really interesting jobs externally, what kept me here was the culture. We have strong policies on enabling people and investing lots in training and developing people into their next roles. The intent is to make people feel that they will gain more by staying and growing than by leaving. It's a very creative place to work.'**

The opportunity to shape a business culture and to embed core values throughout an organisation to achieve business results was key to their vision of driving business performance strategies.

> **'My approach to combining the two cultures in one of the factories is driven by values.'**

> **'It's important to have the opportunity to try and change an organisation's values in line with my own.'**

> **'My drivers are continuing to grow, a desire to achieve, an opportunity to impose my values or realign those of the organisation.'**

'In a sense it is too paternalistic an organisation – it's very financially successful but is a little bit too paternalistic. I like there to be individual recognition as well as collective.'

Value conflict

Where their own values had conflicted with those of colleagues or the organisation, this gave rise to conflict or precipitated a move to another role or business. The women were realistic enough to know that a 100% match throughout a career would be nigh on impossible to achieve, but a close identification with corporate values played a significant part in the level of job satisfaction. An understanding of how closely aligned those values were then opened up a series of choices around how to address differences should there be any.

'My values are never in conflict here because I'm the boss but it was an issue at my previous organisation. You find a way of accommodating those conflicts and if you can't my choice would be to leave and move on. If your personal values are constantly compromised and that's important to you, then you should move on.'

'When my values have not been aligned, I have tackled it head on, agreeing to differ sometimes.'

'That business was very hire and fire and very political. If your face fitted, you were okay. I disliked that – it didn't inspire any loyalty.'

'There came a point where I thought to myself these guys aren't worth working with – let's move on. It was time to move on anyway – there was no natural place to go on to.'

'Yes, my values have been in conflict – if you can't stand the heat, get out of the kitchen. I know why the organisation has taken a position – I can either manage it through as best as I can or stick to my principles and it happens anyway – what does it achieve? I know I should take a particular decision but it gets changed at a different level so you have to try and influence it differently (i.e. how the decision gets implemented). If you really think 'this is a terrible organisation' you really shouldn't stay – there are other jobs you could do.'

Leading by example

A high sense of personal integrity and strong personal credibility underlines the value set and is intrinsic to the way these women lead their organisations. Treating people as they would like to be treated and remembering the bad as well as the good examples was an instructive approach.

'I try to lead by example – e.g. I would never travel business class if other people in the party were travelling economy.'

'I tell people here that they are the most important thing for them – you're only as good as your last job. I could get booted out tomorrow and that's the deal nowadays.'

'I was given an acting role for a while before I was made MD – it gave me time to establish confidence and credibility so I was happy to bide my time.'

'I've seen people promoted past me and I try to remember not to behave like some of those I was promoted past. One

person wouldn't work with me, one tried to undermine me, one tried to scupper projects by deliberately missing deadlines. It ended up being worse for them than it was for me. It's a mistake to let things eat you up like that.'

'I'm there to go to battle for the team when needed or help in times of crisis. I've never had to ask for a pay rise and I don't believe other people should have to.'

'I learned to have the courage of my conviction. You should treat other people as you would like to be treated. I liked to learn and always wanted a challenge. I liked to make my own rules and be myself. Recognition is key to the environment I wanted to create. My role is to create shareholder value and the management team does the rest.'

These comments underline research that demonstrates that women score higher on transformational leadership than their male counterparts. In a rapidly changing business environment charged with uncertainty and shorter periods of employment where competitive advantage is increasingly based upon knowledge workers, winning the hearts and minds of the people who make the business successful is critical.

A rewarding role

The sense of reward and achievement for these women was less about status, kudos and money than about delivering results and again feeling like they were adding value and making a difference.

'Women are more multi-faceted than men – I don't really care who wins or loses but I am hell-bent on delivering.'

'The money's good but I would never do anything just for the money.'

'I love taking the business forward, seeing things evolve. We've just launched a new product which came from something I saw when I was visiting a supplier almost three years ago and it's been very successful – that gives you a real thrill.'

'We have made huge progress and I get tremendous satisfaction from seeing things through – and they're all long-term initiatives at this level.'

'A desire to achieve. A desire to learn. I wanted to be in a position where I could influence the business.'

'I find it motivating to see the business and organisation improve. We don't have shareholders so we have to work a bit harder at driving the company as there isn't the market pressure and intellectually that's quite challenging.'

One of the most important factors cited in terms of value fit with the organisation was the person that they were working for and this played a key role in whether potential new roles were accepted or not. Shared values and an opportunity to learn generated the respect necessary for a productive working relationship.

'There comes a point where you recognise that you can't work with the person interviewing you and you'll decline the job, however interesting the job is. It's a people game – that's what work is about. If you can't interact with the people around you it's a non-starter for me.'

'I work for the intellectual challenge and to have good people to work with. It's interesting and difficult.'

'The interesting thing looking back – whoever I worked for (with the exception of one or two) I have always made it my business to get on very well with my boss – it's crucially important who you work for, who you give your commitment and your loyalty to. It has to be somebody and it has to be the person you report to – if you don't get on with the person you report to then move because you have to have somebody who's your champion. The boss has to be somebody you respect. If you don't have that I think you're wasting your time. I could never ever work for someone who I didn't respect, who I couldn't speak to and say what I thought – that for me would be the number one rule.'

Getting the best out of people

Being promoted past peers gave rise to some difficult issues and the most successful approach was to constructively tackle the conflict rather than ignore it or manage the individuals out of the way. Again, a focus on development, getting the best out of people and giving people the chance to change was the preferred option where possible.

'I like to have things out in the open. I did have an issue when a peer became a subordinate. So I raised the topic with him – 'Have we got an issue here? You need to tell me how you feel and how we can move this forward positively.' One individual left as he couldn't cope with working for a woman. Another became one of my managers – it took two years to work it through but I now

count him as one of my best friends. There's lots of mutual respect now.'

Some however were somewhat less subtle in their approach but recognised that in themselves and the impact that that might have on their profile and progress.

'My way of dealing with someone who is being difficult or unconstructive is not necessarily the cleverest way because I'm very outspoken about them being a waste of space – of course, if you say that, you raise questions.'

Nowhere is the challenge to values clearer than when these women have come up against discrimination. Having being brought up to believe that they were as good as anyone else, and that they were capable of achieving their goals, being confronted by overt or covert sexism is something that many had needed to come to terms with and learn to deal with. Most have tempered their response over time, becoming more secure in their position and value to the organisation, preferring instead to focus on the bigger issues at hand.

'There were some clients who had a problem with me because I was a woman and I was always being mistaken for a secretary but internally that just became a joke rather than an issue. By and large I can give as good as I get – I don't take it too seriously now – I've grown out of that. Occasionally I'll rise to it. Now there are a lot of younger male colleagues who have wives who work and so understand. If I really felt it was a genuine reluctance I would take it very much more seriously.'

'I have sometimes come up against more blatant sexism

but you have to make a judgement as to whether it's worth the power struggle – there are bigger issues to think about when you are running a business.'

'I'm much more tolerant than some of the younger women I see – perhaps I shouldn't be. I see that they are not prepared to make so many compromises and that's good.'

'I've always been focused on doing a job rather than building a career, therefore early on I wasn't perceived to be a threat to men.'

Is it worth it?

A strong sense of values is what typically underpinned decisions to accept or reject roles and the consequent trade-offs that they might involve. Clarity around what they were really in it for enabled a clearer evaluation of organisations and roles however tempting the offers might be.

'I don't see my children as much as I would like but I can control that much more than other people.'

'My husband would like me to give up work so we could do lots of things together. I have girlfriends who don't work and in the summer play tennis, go to London, have lunch and I wonder what I'm doing, but I wouldn't have it any different.'

A recognition that the values and trade-off decisions would change over time was also seen as being important and it was important to keep sight of this to keep work and life on track throughout their careers.

**'Be prepared to constantly reassess your priorities and
what your values are. There are critical stages in both your
personal and professional life when you have to
fundamentally reassess and this covers work, partner,
kids and so on. I've seen other people choose to
downshift. Flexibility of mind is all important.'**

This mindset also plays to the flexible approach to career paths
advocated in Chapter Three. Too rigid a life plan makes it very
difficult to accommodate changes in outlook, priorities and
circumstances, some of which may be beyond an individual's
control. Values and beliefs may change with experience in the
same way as ambitions and priorities, and therefore the ability
to objectively assess the options and to be big enough to change
direction if appropriate is a real asset.

... Key Points ...

- Be clear about what's important to you – what does your personal set of values look like? What are your real motivators?

- Be true to yourself.

- If your values don't fit with the organisation and they matter to you then you're unlikely to be happy there. Be prepared to move if you're not in a position to influence them.

- Treat others as you would like to be treated.

- Be realistic. Be prepared to recognise that your priorities and values may change and be big enough to admit and accommodate that.

Chapter Eight

The Next Generation

So what perceptions do the young women have who are entering the workplace now? Selected for their work experience, career focus and academic achievements, the undergraduates interviewed had quite a broad awareness of the realities that lay ahead. In comparison to those graduating only ten years ago, they appeared much more streetwise about their prospects. In the main however, they felt that those of their friends who had not had prior work experience had an unrealistic outlook and were in for a surprise when they started out on their careers.

What was interesting was the level of awareness of the issues that faced them and the striking parallels with some of the senior women interviewed. Academically strong and accustomed to performing well, they still felt the weight of expectation and pressure to be successful.

During their work experience, they had seen the politics of

the workplace, the importance of organisational culture and the subtly different rules applied to men and women. They had become aware of the importance of profile and networking and had come to realise what was important to them when choosing a career. What was also surprising was that, in general, careers were being considered in terms of their long-term appeal and options, not just the immediate prospects. Some had been assigned mentors (both good and bad) and had seen the value of having someone show you the unwritten rules and how to get yourself noticed and recognised.

Aspirations

Whilst none had clear career plans in terms of the level of seniority they were aspiring to they did have some clear ideas about what would be important to them and what would motivate them to do well. Pragmatism in terms of wanting to earn enough to be able to do the things they wanted to do was mixed with a desire to be able to 'have a life' or have more flexibility. None of them was motivated by the money in itself which was interesting, given the recent levels of student debt reported as being anywhere between £5,000 and £12,000 upon graduation.

> **'I don't have a long-term goal to be running a company by the time I'm 40. I need to be earning enough to support me and I want it to be a satisfying job.'**

> **'I would much rather be in a job that I enjoy than in a better paid job that I don't like.'**

> **'Money isn't my primary driver although I am aware of what a difference it can make as my parents are not as comfortably off as they were.'**

'The priority wasn't the money – I could never be a trader, I would hate it. It was definitely the people and the feedback from the work I did in research that was very positive. It's difficult to think that far ahead – I really don't know where I'll be in a few years. I don't think I want to live in London – I would like to have a family and I don't think I would want that in London.'

In parallel with their older counterparts, the strong motivator for these undergraduates was doing the very best they could and enjoying the challenges at hand.

'I've always been pretty ambitious and wanted the image of having a successful job – a personal sense of having achieved and that I've done something that's difficult to do. The money helps and I thrive on stress but ultimately I wouldn't do anything unless I was enjoying it.'

'I want to be the best I can at what I enjoy and I'll do it as long as I enjoy it. I don't have a plan and I don't believe in one employer for life.'

'It gives me satisfaction to know that I've surprised people with how well I've done but long-term, it's about looking after my family.'

The attitudes expressed during these interviews reflect some of the forecasts made in the Foresight Report in that none of the young women were looking at a job or career for life. They were keen to be learning and to be enjoying what they were doing but did not anticipate being in the same type of company or even necessarily in the same area longer term.

'I'm interested long-term in setting up an independent

business. It's only really occurred to me recently that I could set up my own business because I've never known anyone who's done it so I never thought I could do it.'

'Ten years or so from now I want a job that allows me to grow but I don't want to sacrifice everything else to be good at this. I want to learn and not get bored but I want a life. The whole package is interesting – money isn't everything. After a certain point, the marginal cost of getting that extra money is just not worth it.'

'Now we take jobs as they come – if we enjoy it then it's great and if we don't then we just move on. Things are a lot more flexible and I don't feel the pressure to do a job that's forever.'

'At some point, I think it would be attractive to have my own company and do things the way I want to – I've met some women who have done that and they've done really well.'

A balanced view

In some instances, parental experiences had provided insights into the trade-offs that some individuals make both good and bad and this had an influence on their outlook. For others, family figures have set precedents for their own ambitions and have partially defined their expectations of themselves.

'I'm interested in doing well and being the best I can be at the job I'm doing, I'm not interested in making millions. Money is important to lead a certain lifestyle but only to a point. I'm not prepared to work 14 hours a day. There's no point in ruining health for the rest of your life in order to do well at your job. I'm not going to put myself in that position as I don't think it's worth it.'

'Dad has been quite formative. He used to take me on business trips, introducing people to me and explaining things to me – it means I have a better understanding of what it's all about. It's really helped me understand what I think I want to do.'

'I come from a family where men and women went to university and did whatever they wanted.'

'I've never questioned graduating and getting a good job. My parents run their own business. What's really surprising is that both my grandmothers had their own businesses as well and they were quite strong characters.'

This awareness of possibilities and potential difficulties can only serve to be of benefit to the younger women in the future.

The right place for me

Exposure to different styles and cultures had already defined for some the type of business they did or did not want to be part of. Though in the main they were entering male-dominated sectors, they were aware of the different types of environment that suited them and their style, and the value of having a network of female colleagues within them. Fitting in and feeling part of the organisation was key to how they felt about the organisations and in this respect their female colleagues had generally made more of an effort to understand any concerns they might have and help them to be successful.

'I did find that it was generally the women who were nicest to me – they took the most interest in me. Partly that was because they had more time – they weren't running the department. I got the impression that that was to do with family and the fact that men don't have to have babies and were able to rise through the ranks quicker. The other place I worked at had lots of women with families and that was very much the culture.'

'It was useful having a female mentor who was fantastic. She took me on all her jobs during my internship and I got loads of exposure to lots of deals and I don't think I would have got the job otherwise. She made sure I got the best experience. I got to meet loads of people. It was good to see senior women there who are well thought of. I got to understand how it all works.'

Having had some work experience, they were better able to identify the organisational cultures that would suit them. In general, their preference was for collaborative, team-based environments.

'Different companies have different cultures – some don't realise that people are people and they don't treat them like people. Some of them look miserable and yet they think we're impressed because of the job they do.'

'I prefer a cooperative environment rather than a competitive environment.'

'It's a team environment. There's an element of competitiveness amongst the people who join at the same time but it's not aggressive.'

'My driver is doing something I'm interested in but having the freedom to do it as I want.'

'A lot of the women said they found research a lot more conducive – quieter and more work-oriented. Research is more team focused.'

Measures of success

When asked what they thought would determine their success in their chosen careers, they displayed little naiveté, their work experience having served to show them what really makes the difference.

'Success will be how well I do the job but a large element will be who you know and how well you know them and I don't know how good I'll be at that.'

'I think it will be a question of looking for opportunities and proving that I can do the job. I think I'll have to make myself quite visible which isn't something that comes naturally to me. I've learned from watching people that I'll have to be very pushy.'

'It's the people who made themselves get noticed who get the jobs.'

'Early on success will be exams, later on it will be: have you done the right work and done the right thing, have you made the right impression on clients. I don't think it relies upon the personal impression of any one person. Later on, the relationship with the partners will help. It will change depending upon what level you're at.'

'Performance in fund management is really clear cut – there's not as much room for discrimination – there's less need for self-promotion because it's obvious how well you've done or not.'

None of them felt particularly comfortable with the prospect of networking and self-promotion to get themselves recognised but adopted a pragmatic view that it was a necessary evil if other people were going to get ahead because of it.

Their own judgement on what they would feel to be success was, like their older colleagues, driven by values rather than a particular place in the hierarchy or the trappings of status. None of them saw themselves as being the one of the next generation of business leaders.

'Success will be how confident I'm feeling and how happy and contented I am. I'm not pushy enough to be head of chambers as they are mostly men or extremely driven women.'

'There are other jobs that I could probably do but I would have to try really hard and probably wouldn't enjoy it. I don't think it's just a pure skill thing – it's more what is required to be successful – some investment and consulting jobs are very masculine, you have to fight and be aggressive – that's not really what I want.'

Under pressure

Having been high performers academically, they felt that there was an expectation that they would go on to have high-flying careers and that in some cases their peers were dissuaded from doing what they really wanted to do as it wasn't seen to have high-flying status. This they felt was a mistake as you're as unlikely to be successful doing something you don't really want to do as you're unlikely to enjoy it.

'Better to go and do what you want rather than to do something you feel you should do and then end up jacking it in to do what you really want to do – that's crazy.'

'There's always an underlying pressure from school that you're bright and you should go and do great things. I think there's a bit of a backlash – three of my close friends have just decided to be teachers and had some concerns about whether this was what was expected of them, but they have decided to do it anyway.'

'Some of those taken in by it all now don't like it but face taking a pay cut if they want to go and do something else, so they feel trapped. It's a mistake to be attracted by the highest paying jobs. They want graduates to think it's really glam and a great deal but why do they have to sell so hard if it's that good?'

'You feel the pressure of going on to a high performing job – a friend who became a teacher was made to feel like she couldn't get a proper job when it's what she actually really wanted to do.'

Despite a track record of doing well and performing at a high level, the undergraduates displayed the same self-doubt and high degree of self-awareness that was characteristic of their more senior counterparts.

'I'm very aware of what I don't know as well as what I do

and it can be very useful but it makes you a bit anxious. I consider myself a bit of an all-rounder – that makes me doubt my abilities to be the best at anything. I'm good at juggling lots of things. I wonder whether other women feel the same. I don't doubt my abilities to be a juggler and be a productive worker.'

'I'm slightly concerned that I lack competitive ambition – I don't consider myself to be a competitive person but I think I hold myself back. I don't think I'll be backstabbingly ambitious.'

'I worried about my financial analysis being in presentations to clients. I think most people who are quite driven are very self-critical and it might be a bit of a woman thing.'

'You're less conscious of your strengths than you are of your weaknesses – your strengths you take for granted because you can do them and you don't give yourself credit.'

Not such a modern world

Having been brought up to believe that they were competing on an equal basis and would be treated the same as their male colleagues, it had been a shock to some to encounter some extremely old-fashioned treatment from male colleagues.

'I wasn't comfortable with all the innuendos in the working environment and I'd never experienced that before – I didn't see why I should have to put up with it. In the pubs, I can get up and walk away. In the work environment, it's different.'

'One of the women was wearing a dark aubergine suit and was told to change. I had been warned but I was still a bit surprised by the reality of it.'

'I was very glad of having a female mentor. There's not many of you and it can be quite difficult. It's harder to get along with people – they can be very patronising. I was working with a male gap year student and he didn't have the same issues.'

'I was very conscious when we were socialising because they were all lads – they often had plans together and that could be difficult.'

For young women emerging from education where their achievements and abilities have been recognised in an equal way to their fellow male students, this obviously came as a surprise.

So, they are under no illusions that while many things have changed, there is still a long way to go.

So how do they think they will cope? They understand that these things will take time to change and they will have to find a way to manage it so that it does not inhibit their success, whatever they choose to do.

'I'm under no illusion that it will change radically or quickly but I think I'm okay with that and I can handle it quite well.'

'It was quite difficult and I realised that if I couldn't deal with it I wasn't going to be successful.'

'You have to continue to challenge men and show that you can consistently perform as well. There's still an attitude

that 'look at that and she's a woman'. You need to know how other people manage difficult situations.'

People to talk to

Having had work experience, they acknowledged that it's useful to have insights from other women within the businesses or careers they choose to pursue.

'It's definitely useful to talk to a woman rather than a bloke especially those who have families. It's interesting to see things from a woman's point of view – especially those older women who had quite a tough time and who are aware of how much it has changed or not, as most men probably think it's pretty equitable now.'

However, prior to having had work experience, they felt it would be difficult to take advantage of that network as they would not have expected to need it, believing that the rules were exactly the same whatever their gender. They felt that without work experience they would not have understood or accepted a need to talk to other women, as they would not have recognised the issues.

'It would be difficult for successful role models to talk to young women now as, without work experience, undergraduates are likely to say 'We don't need it. We know what we're doing' because they haven't been out there yet. They also wouldn't know what questions to ask.'

'My awareness has come from having work experience – prior to that I didn't think there would be an issue.'

'It was only once I started working that I became aware of it.'

Careers and children

Even at this early stage, the undergraduates were, for the most part, considering the challenges of combining a family with a career. Some had mothers who had had careers, others had worked part-time and others had not worked. They all expected their partners to take an equal share in household responsibilities and felt that they would probably be trying to manage dual careers. They were under no illusions however that it would be easy to attain a satisfactory balance of managing a career and a family.

'I can't envisage myself not having children but I can't yet work out how that's going to work. So many more people are being single mothers – there are so many people I've met who have divorced parents. So many people who are potential role models have ended up as single mums, which worries me.'

'It's always going to be a problem that women will be regarded as a risk as they may go off and have babies. Not all women will want to come back and you can't predict that. You have to be aware that things are different. The tendency for people to get married later also changes the way organisations are as they expect single person commitment until you're 30 and if that doesn't fit, then it's difficult.'

These interviews with bright, talented young women about to embark upon their careers serve to illustrate that the value of work experience is far greater than a simple understanding of a particular job or sector and how little some things have changed. There are more senior women in business today and organisations are recognising the value that women can bring, yet there are still clearly cultures, behaviours and expectations from society that continue to raise issues for the current generation. Potentially the gap between their expectations and reality is even greater as most women who have done well at school and university do not even question their right to compete equally with men as that is what they have been raised to do. Equally this may be a positive thing as it means that they will be more demanding, less tolerant and more challenging of any inequalities they encounter. It's not a question of feminism, 'women's lib' or glass ceilings. It's simply a need for those women to understand the reality and how best to manage it so that it doesn't inhibit them, and for organisations to figure out how to get the best performances out of their employees whatever their gender.

... Key Points ...

- Today's undergraduates appear more street-wise about the realities of the work environment.

- They are more demanding in terms of work-life balance and less accepting of any gender differences.

- Those without work experience may have unrealistic perceptions.

- Their motivators and concerns are the same as the women who went before them.

- They recognise the value of having other women to talk to.

Chapter Nine

A Bird's Eye View

The senior women interviewed for this book clearly combine a wealth of experience and insights. Whilst they have all seen significant developments for women in the workplace, not least marked by their own successes, they recognise that the pressures of education and society have changed and that some of the issues remain as difficult now as they were twenty years ago. They have witnessed significant changes in the number of women in their organisations and industries over time. However, they still see a lack of women applying for more senior roles and less traditional female roles such as engineering and technology.

'When I got promoted, my role was advertised in the press. There was a huge number of applicants but hardly any women and none who made the long list. It's a shame

really. There are still many areas where women still haven't broken through.'

Compounding the problem is a lack of appropriate role models for young professional women entering the workplace. This was highlighted as a concern by the women interviewed as, in their view, expectations are higher, the image of the 'superwoman' is unreal and unhelpful and in most cases the young women are not well prepared for the realities of the working environment.

That it should still merit comment when a woman reaches a Board level position is an indication that, although some things have changed since these women started out, there are still many more changes to come. This was commented upon recently by Dame Stella Rimington in her book 'Open Secret'. Since retiring from the Intelligence Service she has entered the world of commerce and industry and was somewhat surprised at what she found.

'I was frankly amazed to be told by the Chairmen of several companies, "We need a woman on the Board". It was clear that those Chairman did not much care what woman, nor did they perceive that 'a woman' might have just as much to contribute as 'a man', and that she would certainly be just as different from another woman as she would be from a man. And I was astounded when the Chairman of one British plc said to me, 'I think we need a woman on the Board, but I am afraid I would not be able to persuade my fellow Directors of that.'

Most of the women interviewed did not feel well prepared for the world of work when they embarked upon their careers and they still perceive this to be an issue today.

'It's a concern that some of the younger women may look at the more senior ones and think that 'they're superhuman' and that 'I can't do that' because there still aren't very many – they are all very strong women. Some of them are in roles which are very unpredictable, not many of them have children (that's a much more worrying statistic) and a number of them are divorced.'

'When I came out of university, I thought I could do anything – that's why you don't give graduates proper jobs. University isn't at all vocational and shouldn't be. The macho stuff crept up on me – it's more a case of realising that you can fit in but you can make a choice not to. Work is about a growing sense of self-worth and self-value.'

This was, to some degree, borne out by the interviews with the undergraduates as they felt that their friends who had not yet had any work experience had no idea about the realities of the working environment.

Equally they felt that whilst there are more women entering the workforce there are still large areas of business where, for a number of reasons, they are not applying.

'One of the biggest disappointments for me is the lack of women applying for and qualified for jobs in the technology sector – I think they check out too early and it's worse here than in the States – some of the decisions girls are making early on preclude some of the options later on. "I'll be a nurse then I can have kids etc." – you just decided not to be a doctor.'

Interviews with the undergraduates and professional and personal knowledge of women at various stages of their careers reveal that many of the issues remain the same as those experienced by the senior women, whilst others are subtly different. Instead of feeling as though they are trailblazers that have to succeed for the women coming through behind them, they feel that they owe it to the trailblazers to follow their success, to be advancing their careers at the same time as embarking upon motherhood.

Having been educated to achieve, they feel a certain pressure to go on and do great things and take the opportunities in front of them in both the personal and professional arenas. Expectations of themselves are high and they feel increasing and competing pressures. For some, that pressure is to stay at home when they wish to work, for others, it's a pressure to combine careers and motherhood because 'that's what successful career women do'.

The women I see choosing to combine careers with motherhood have, in general, chosen to return to work (some for four days a week) and they all have partners who take some share of domestic responsibilities. Yet how many of their partners would also have been able to return for four days a week? Society itself has not changed sufficiently for another pattern to be easily acceptable and for most men to be able to consider the same flexible working arrangements, even if that might be their preferred option. In the same way that female directors attract press comments, men who take on the bulk of the childcare are equally newsworthy. The messages that are sent out about careers, family values and achievement are, for many, confusing.

What struck me most about the women interviewed for this work is that they have not waited for business and society to change. They have set their own expectations and rules, recognised that there needs to be some flexibility throughout and have not allowed other people's expectations and prejudices to stand in their way.

> **'If you go on about the glass ceiling, you are in danger of becoming ghettoised. Recognise that women are still in a minority and do what you can to proactively manage and support.'**

In the main, success was not a conscious plan – it was simply the way it turned out and most have had the support of their partner, friends and family. One of the clearest messages that came from these women is that if you want to be fulfilled at home as well as at work, you cannot do it all by yourself – something will give, be it your health, your career or your relationships, so avoid the temptation to try to be superwoman. Be realistic enough to know what you're good at and be big enough to ask for help with the rest. That self-awareness and ability to recognise talent in others will stand you in good stead.

Another big message that came through loud and clear was learning to define for yourself what success looked like. You can be successful in someone else's model but you're unlikely to be happy doing it if the measures of success and the values by which they operate are different to your own. A confidence in your ability to achieve and a strong sense of your own personal values can carry you a long way and will carry you through the bad as well as the good times. If, in the long term, the things that will make you proud are not the things that the organisation values, then you're in the wrong place. Have the courage of your convictions and look for other opportunities that will be a better fit.

None of the women here presumed to have all the answers or to have found the right way of dealing with everything. Indeed the nature of their particular industries, personal circumstance and individual personalities meant that what worked well for one would probably not have worked for another.

It seems to me that one of the biggest messages to take away is to always try and keep options open for yourself. Even if you don't use them, you will always feel in a stronger position if you can make choices about what you do and don't want to do. Being aware of the implications of the decisions you make is important but at the end of the day the decisions you make have to be best for you and anyone else they involve.

Important decisions such as whether and how to try and combine dual careers and parenthood are, at the end of the day, down to you and your partner, so worry less about what other people think and make sure you make the right decision for you.

It's reassuring to know that these tremendously successful and capable women have all had concerns and crises of confidence, they have all found the need for people to talk to, and they have not had a highly structured path to get to where they are now. They see the same issues of lack of confidence and self-belief mirrored in the women coming through behind them and they see helping with that as one of their greatest responsibilities.

'The most important thing I can do for other women in this company is to do well in the job and make the company do well. I do more mentoring with the more senior women. I see the issues of confidence with those that are ten years younger than me. Those that are 20 years younger come out and expect the world to be at their feet and have very clear plans. Work isn't like that.

The way you develop and respond to the situations you're put in is very dynamic and you don't know what skills you might find you have or roles you like. I try hard

to counter lack of confidence by encouraging people to believe in their own abilities.'

Whilst many women may choose not to pursue high-flying careers, those who do should find some comfort in the insights shared here which reveal the women to be immensely human and not the 'superwoman' myths that unsettle us all.

No doubt business and society will continue to change. Indeed a growing awareness of the strengths of women as transformational leaders and the forecast change in working patterns may mean that the really smart and successful organisations will learn how to understand the different motivators and strengths of their male and female colleagues and use them all to their full. Adopting a one-size-fits-all approach to individuals in a knowledge based economy would seem to be fundamentally flawed. These changes are however likely to take some time to develop so, in the meantime, it is down to each individual to take control of her own career, aspirations and lifestyle and do what she believes to be right for her. Through sharing their experiences women can provide valuable networks for their female peers and may even find themselves acting as role models for future generations. So take control, consider your options and most of all, be true to yourself.

And Finally ...
a Few Words from Those Who Know...

The final stage of the interviews was to ask the women to reflect and to summarise the key pieces of advice that they would like to pass on to the generations of women coming through behind them. What follows is a selection of the most common themes and advice.

Manufacturing

- Be realistic about what you, as an individual, can achieve in terms of your intrinsic skills not your qualifications.
- Be pushy.

Healthcare

- Take control and embrace change.
- If you really don't like an organisation, then leave.
- Treat people like people.

- Be flexible and be prepared to work at it.

Marketing Consultancy

- Act like a colleague and people will treat you like a boss.
- The most painful mistakes can be the most memorable and useful.
- Don't be affected by other people's perceptions – define success for yourself and know when you've got it.

Media

- Focus 95% on the job and 5% on your PR within the organisation.
- Learn beyond the job you're doing.
- Don't pick someone who will be easy to manage – pick the best you can and that will create a really strong team.

PR

- Be prepared to say you've made a mistake.
- Don't believe that most things are impossible.
- Do something you like in an atmosphere that you like.
- Create opportunities – don't sit and wait for things to happen.

Manufacturing

- Never say never – keep as many options open as you can.
- Recognise you might not always make the right decision but its important to feel that it was the right thing to do at the time.

- You have to believe in what you're doing.

Media

- Don't think about glass ceilings – don't look for reasons why not.

- Being aware that it's different for women can be really helpful.

- Take advantage of the fact that there's no reference point so you can make your own rules.

PR

- Don't expect nothing will change when you have kids.

- Apply the same rules to everyone whatever level they are.

- Don't let the scale of a role faze you.

Manufacturing

- Always rise to any challenge.

- Don't accept a glass ceiling – sometimes we put it there ourselves.

- If your employer doesn't recognise you go somewhere else.

Publishing

- Everything's possible.

- Don't be scared to change your mind.

- Responsibility is taken never given.

- Do it now – don't wait.

Retail

- Play to your strengths and use your team to complement your weaknesses.

- Think about what's important to you so you can see when it's off-track.

- Stay true to your values even if you have conflicting advice.

Technology

- Be very ambitious – assume you will need to over-achieve.

- Get a skill, get educated, work hard and then get on with it.

- Don't feel you have to behave like a man.

Media

- Never do anything if you don't think it's going to be fun and you're not going to enjoy it.

Professional services

- Choose an area that's of interest to you.

- Be prepared to be committed – if you're not go somewhere else.

- Choose the right partner – you can't do it without.

FMCG

- Always go for jobs that are interesting and attract you in terms of their challenge.

- Try to work for people that are really going places, that you admire and can learn from. You can learn from a poor boss but not as much as you can from a good one.

- Keep on educating yourself.

Professional services

- Find a mentor or someone you can trust and will never betray your confidence – don't take a chance on someone.

- Believe in yourself and have the courage of your convictions and behave according to your beliefs – stick to your values.

Retail

- Find a mentor who will never betray your confidence.

- Have the courage of your convictions and behave according to your beliefs.

- Collaborate – work not as an individual but as part of a tight-knit team.

Index